Dear Reader,

So much has happened in the coaching field in the last 10 months since the Limited Beta Edition of this book came out.

There are now many places you can go to create a product, to learn about the internet as a coach, even to hire someone to do it all for you. Choice is a great thing, isn't it?

What this says to me is that the Multiple Streams Business Model for Coaches has come of age with grace and endurance.

More and more coaches are proving beyond reasonable doubt that this is a viable, meaningful and above all sustainable way to deliver coaching results to many, and enjoy the rewards of being a successful coach.

Because of this, the world has changed. It's a better place and I'm so glad.

I hope you enjoy Multiple Streams of Coaching Income, the 2nd Edition, which you now hold in your hands. It's been made more robust (and several chapters longer) with the help of coaches like you from around the world.

It's my fervent wish that you'll drink it in, let it feed your boldest dreams, and come back to it often. Most of all, I trust you'll continue to urgently pursue a coaching approach to everything you touch.

Here's to meaning and money for all coaches!

Love,

Andrea

Acclaim for "Multiple Streams of Coaching Income"

As a result of Multiple Streams of Coaching Income, I invested 10 hours developing my first serious e-product. Four weeks later it generated $30,000 in profit in 10 days.

CHRIS BARROW

The Dental Business School

www.dentalbusinessschool.com

Yesterday... I had not one, but TWO new clients sign up for coaching after going through my pink spoon e-course at www.musicbizcoaching.com. Until switching to "one-banana," I never had someone just sign up for coaching online. It works!

JOE TAYLOR JR.

Taylor Creative Management

www.spinme.com

Multiple Streams of Coaching Income is more than a book. It's a deep tissue coaching experience. Engaging calls to action connect me sustainably with money and meaning. I'm now leveraging what I have into more than I imagined possible.

SYLVIA WARREN, MBA

www.simplythebestcoaching.com

Multiple Streams of Coaching Income author Andrea Lee is one of the most internet marketing savvy individuals I have ever met. She is in tune, not only with what people need, want and will buy, but what our ecology needs, what our humanity needs, even what our fellow species need.

ANNA DARGITZ, PhD
Certified Coach
former Dean of Students
Graduate School of Coaching
www.advancedcommunicating.com

Andrea Lee has been an invaluable gem for me in building my own virtual business. Andrea knows the ins and outs of running an on-line business, and doing with so with grace, courage, and heart.

NINA EAST
Certified Coach
www.MyMentorCoach.com
www.NinaEast.com

This is the book the coaching industry has needed for a decade. Reading this book will set you free to make the money you deserve as a professional. Andrea gives us permission to associate the word M O N E Y and coaching in a powerful and uplifting way.

ROBERT ALDERMAN, MCC, CPBA
www.performanceprofiles.com

It's just past 4am and I'm up at my desk. You have woken me up. It's this darned book of yours. I have read the first 60 or so pages and I'm fed up of nodding 'Yes, yes, yes!'. Now that I've got that off my chest, I need to go back to bed...if I can sleep. If I can't...what a way to keep awake!"

MARTIN HAWORTH
Director of Development, UK-ICF
www.coaching-businesses-to-success.com

I know I'm a big gushing dork, but I keep reading random pages of the book and it is awesome. It is so great, Andrea. I'm serious. I hope you're celebrating!

ANDY WIBBELS
Author of *BlogWild!*
www.sixfigureblogging.com

Not since the days of Thomas Leonard has there been such a bold, incisive look into the future of coaching - or such a clearly delineated roadmap to get us from here to there.

BARRY ZWEIBEL, PCC,
GottaGettaCoach!, Inc.

Multiple Streams of Coaching Income is a must read for all life coaches, authors and speakers who want to play on a bigger stage by more effectively leveraging their time, money, energy and other resources.

BONITA JOY YODER
Author of *Invest Like a Millionaire and Sleep Like an Angel! A Spiritual Guide to the Heart and Soul of Real Estate Investing*

Andrea, I've been teaching the Multiple Streams material to the Virtual Assistant market for a few months now and I'm loving it! I didn't have to create the content myself, but yet I have a whole program to teach at my fingertips - and a great, easy to follow program at that! This means my work credibility and substance, very quickly, has enabled me to focus on other parts of my product funnel ... Other products that I can quickly create, building the list and actually delivering great value to my clients.

I really recommend it to other business owners who want to bypass some of the product creation process and look fantastice to their niche!
CINDY GREENWAY
www.multiplestreamsteam.com

Andrea Lee gives you an incredible range of support to extend your work to clients you haven't even imagined yet -and the package comes with empathy, humor and necessary technical details.
LAURIE WEISS, PH.D., MCC
Author of *What is the Emperor Wearing?*
Truth-Telling in Business Relationships.
www.RelationshipHQ.com

"A much needed resource in a profession which is finally waking up to the fact that a successful coaching business needs a decent income, and that this takes work. This book shows us how."
COEN DE GROOT
www.CoachCoen.com
www.EuroCoachList.com

A must for ANY coach who has the space for some more income. Andrea, or 'A' as she is affectionately known, has used her extensive knowledge and experience of the coaching market to bring to the profession a very important book.

STEVE STOCKTON, CEO
www.24-7coaching.com

After I read the first chapter of this book, I noticed I was hardly breathing. Finally, someone was telling my truth - that it's hard to make money as a coach. By the second chapter, I was smiling and filled with hope. This book provides specific strategies that will transform struggling, broke coaches into successful and prosperous coaches. The best part is that it really works!

LYNNE KLIPPEL, MOT, OTR/L, CCC
author of *Secrets to Surviving HIS Job Loss*
Web Wonder Women
www.LynneKlippel.com

This book sets a new heartfelt business standard for the coaching profession. We have much more to give the world and Andrea shows the way to mine the vast richness at our feet.

JIMM HUGHEY, M.S.
Love & Wealth Coach
Past President ICF OC

This book is a real 'How To' Manual that shares a proven coaching-approach to success. It couldn't have come at a better time in the coaching industry.

CANDYE HINTON
www.NewCoachesConnection.com
www.CoachingAsYourNextCareer.com

Wow! Prepare to have all your belief systems shifted into high gear. Andrea courageously confronts the limiting concepts standing between Coaches and success, and provides specific guidance on implementing strategies that have all three elements of Greatness: they are Useful, Doable, and Enjoyable.

LABLE BRAUN
www.GuidePrinciples.com

An absolutely brilliant book coming at a critical moment in the coaching profession's evolution. With humor and compassion, Andrea Lee lays out a common sense strategy for helping coaches do what the industry to date has failed to do: teach them to make money.

JUDY MURDOCH, MBA
www.JudyMurdoch.com

In this reader-friendly book, Andrea not only separates the myths from truth, but provides new truths which, if followed, will lead many frustrated coaches to the success they desire. A must-read!

MARCIA BENCH
www.CareerCoachInstitute.com
www.CoachingAndTrainingSolutions.com

Multiple
Streams

OF COACHING INCOME

The Future of Coaching is Now.

ANDREA J. LEE

Published by:
MP Press, an imprint of Femme Osage Publishing
P.O. Box 81
Saint Peters, Missouri, USA 63376
http://www.FemmeOsagePublishing.com

Printed in the United States of America
ISBN: 0-9728940-3-9

Library of Congress Control Number: 2005932680

First Printing 2004
Second Printing 2005
Third Printing 2007

Author Contact:
Andrea J. Lee
Suite 152, 1919B – 4 Street SW
Calgary, AB T2S 1W4
403-615-1237
support@andreajlee.com

Cover design and layout: Cyanotype Book Architects, www.cyanotype.ca

Proofreading: Lynne and Larry Klippel www.femmeosagepublishing.com

THIS BOOK IS DEDICATED TO MICHAEL

Coaching is love made visible. If you can't coach, you can't love.
- ANDREA J. LEE

What the world needs now is love, sweet love...
- BURT BACHARACH

The Most Taboo Subject in Coaching

As you'll soon discover in the following pages, I am rabid about conversations: having them, instigating them, fostering them, multiplying them, and supporting them.

This book is a conversation fire starter about the most taboo topic in coaching: Money, and how to make it.

I believe Multiple Streams of Coaching Income will be the white cue ball on the billiard table—the one that makes a bang as things get under way.

My mission is to put money in the pockets of 10,000 coaches by the year 2008. This book is the start of that and I'm glad you picked it up.

Start reading it at any point. Wherever you look, you'll find a lot of paradigm busters.

The key is to talk about them with someone. As you read, talk over the big and little questions that come up with someone—or with a group of someones.

Since it's a coaching book, it contains a lot of questions that you'll debate. You'll find answers for some and not for others.

Think of the questions you can't answer yet as stimulants in your mind causing you to fire neurons you didn't know you had.

Like bits of sand in an oyster, those questions are the uncomfortable beginnings of new pearls of wisdom for you and for your future as a financially successful coach.

Table of Contents

Preface:
Hungering For a
Vision

Have you ever repotted a plant?

You gently shake the plant and its dirt out of its old home so that you can put it in a bigger container?

Sometimes in doing so you discover that the plant is root-bound... it's been growing for too long in its pot. With no room for additional growth, its roots have become tangled, matted, and grow in circles.

The coaching profession is choking in its own pot.

- - - - - - -

You know how some kids spend the summer holidays at camp, or biking around with friends, slurpees in hand? I remember how much fun they seemed to be having.

Me on the other hand...I was reminded the other day of the year I turned 12 or 13. I spent the summer vacation doing the "books" for my Dad's business.

When school started again in the fall, weekends were special when we got to roll quarters from the laundry machines in Dad's apartment buildings. As a kid, it was weird finding out how really grimy money is.

Rolling quarters is dirty work.

But what made it fun was those rolls of quarters were what bought pizza that night. It was always one Hawaiian and one "all-dressed," from the restaurant across the street on Marine Drive in Vancouver, B.C.

And hey, Mom might have found them heavy to tote, but the quarters were also grocery money.

That's how I grew up. And as I go into my seventh year of running a coaching-related business in summer 2005, I realize I was absolutely never meant for anything else.

As an adult child of an entrepreneur I am so grateful for the way the world looks to me, all filled with possibilities and opportunities, and plenty of bounty for all.

To my Dad, Mom and brothers Eddy and Irwin, I know things are tough right now. I want you to know I care, and I'm as grateful for the gift of you as my family, after all.

To the coaches and entrepreneurs who read this, this is why I do what I do. I'm built with a rabid desire to help businesses like yours bloom, whatever it takes. My passion is for your success.

Why? It comes from caring, deep in the bone, about where courage and the right help can get you...even when you start with rolling quarters.

- - -

Like a plant, when a child grows for too long in its original "container," it becomes root-bound. With no room for additional growth, roots become tangled, matted, and grow in circles.

Root-bound plants and people placed in a larger environment without having their roots untangled often fail to overcome their choked condition. Growth and potential are stunted.

On the other hand, re-potting a plant—or a person—after untangling its roots gives it breathing room for new growth, for new fruit, and for the formation of entire new plants.

That's what this book is about.

Multiple Streams of Coaching Income is a loving repotting of our concept of coaching—from a tight little container into the unbounded earth that provides unlimited opportunity.

And it's just in time.

Multiple Streams was born out of the pain thousands of coaches have expressed about the viability of the coaching profession. "Is the dream dead?" they asked.

From there, it has been driven by a new vision, a huge vision for what the coaching profession can be and do.

Multiple Streams presents a crystal clear vision to coaches that makes the possibilities we've witnessed in the past seem tiny—as though we'd been looking at a single leaf and exclaiming that we beheld a forest.

However, no matter how profound the one-on-one coaching relationship can be, it is not a path to wealth for every coach.

For coaching to survive, we must re-visit and re-think of ways coaching can be delivered to more clients, and can create financial success for more coaches.

So—to continue the analogy—as magnificent as the one *leaf* we knew about has been, the *forest* is what I hope you'll glimpse in the pages of this book.

As you take in the new view that means the most to you, determine to engage your heart and mind in thinking it through. Embrace it.

It's not an overstatement to say that coaching and the coaching approach are more crucial now than ever to human evolution.

For that very reason, we must master financial success as coaches or risk our critical work becoming marginalized, discredited, and just plain ignored.

By drastically opening up our vision of coaching, we 100% un-box the possibilities for our profession in the same way we champion our individual clients.

All of us have lived our entire lives to this point in preparation for the challenges ahead. Will you accept my invitation to become a wealthy, successful, impactful coach?

To lead the way as coaches, we must first be willing to heal ourselves.

To be generous, we must first be wealthy. To give, we must have something TO give. To move, for once and for all, beyond worry about money is to open up our ability to live up to our potential—to do our greatest work.

With you for company, I am excited about the future we will create...starting with our wealth.

Let's stop ignoring the truth and talk about multiple ways for coaches to earn money.

This is about our lives and our livelihoods. Ready, set, engage!

Setting
the
Stage

Why Are You Reading This Book?

Currently, when most coaches are trained, they are encouraged to view coaching as a box:

First, you decide you are a coach. Then you climb into the box.

Once inside, you realize with surprise 'Hey, this box is small.'

When this point first makes it onto your radar, you realize this is NOT what you signed up for.

You are not alone. Here is what some others have said:[*]

- *Even marketing and networking as much as I do, Coaching is really a hard sell. I've become frustrated and have not had a client pay a monthly fee to me in about 6 months. Andrea, I'm very worried that the struggle to find enough paying clients each month will outweigh my passion for, and effectiveness in, coaching. If I'm worried, I know there are hundreds like me and I wonder, "What are we all doing?"*
- *Where are the real live clients?*

- *When I attend the local coaching group, I hear and see that many are scared or frustrated by their lack of clients. It's become upsetting rather than supportive to attend meetings.*
- *Andrea, my first exposure to coaches was when I attended my first coaching association meeting. I felt like the room was full of starving animals and I was fresh meat. I was descended upon by a dozen people hoping they could get me to pay them to let them coach me in something—anything. I left with an almost overwhelming feeling of sadness at their desperation, and almost didn't go back.*
- *I think what we need is for someone to open the gates and let the rest of the population in so we can start coaching THEM instead of each other.*

In other words, coaching as we've known it to date is seen as one thing: coaching one-on-one clients by telephone.

In some circles, that definition may expand to include group coaching, but for the most part the concept of "what a coach does" is limited—and very limiting.

Just like a small box.

The problem with this "small box" that we don't seem to realize is that there is a lot of pain involved in squeezing ourselves into it, and our spirits get bruised.

A few examples?

- the agony of "Am I good enough? Perhaps there's something wrong with me, and that's why I can't make a coaching business work."

- the dejected feeling of having to go back to a "previous life" or career after being chewed up and spit out of the coaching machine.
- the anger at having been "sold" by coach-training organizations.
- the terrible fear, in some cases, that the next business or next endeavor may fail as well.
- the residual effect on spouses and children who ride in the roller coaster as all this works itself out.
- So the sad fact is that many times the only alternative people see to putting up with the box called "coaching" is to get up, walk quickly away, and forget the whole thing.

They determinedly re-learn to ignore the empty feeling of not fulfilling their calling in life. Inexorably, they resign themselves to more pedestrian things.

In this book, what I propose is a more optimistic and realistic view, a dramatically differently view, of what successful coaching looks like.

> # This book is DEFINITELY NOT about a small box.

Coaching is *not* the marketing hamster-wheel from hell. It is *not* a tyrannical schedule filled with hour after hour of one-on-one clients. Coaching is *not* life with a telephone implanted into the side of your head.

What is coaching then? It is helping to create lives that matter using all known methods. Period.

This includes everything: telephone calls, books, memberships, classes, management styles and positions, motivational speaking, videos, CD recordings, and hundreds of other concepts and items. When a person chooses to become a coach, they start a spiritual journey that goes from the thrill of discovery, through a continual process of self-growth and personal evolution, and peaks when all parts are working in harmony towards the main goal.

That is, all parts—mind, body, heart and soul—work with every breath towards a better humanity.

In my heart of hearts, I know this is why you are reading this book. You've told me so yourself, in hundreds of emails like the ones above.

This book is definitely NOT about a small box.

Some of you, especially Members of the *Multiple Streams of Coaching Income* monthly membership, have already begun this new conversation with relish.

> *In less than 60 days after discovering the Multiple Streams of Coaching Income approach, I've completed an e-book, secured a speaking engagement at a national conference, and am developing an extensive audio product.*

> *This information has completely shifted my thinking about my business. I feel less stressed about marketing my 1:1 coaching since I'm creating multiple streams of income. Not surprisingly, I have more 1:1 clients who are attracted to my relaxed marketing approaches.*
> **–LYNNE KLIPPEL**, CoachCorner.com

Andrea, this approach to making money online using a coaching approach is both simple and brilliant. We can take everything we know about coaching and focus it into the online world.

I took one of your suggestions and immediately added it to my own practice. It will make serving clients MUCH easier.
–**DAVID STOWELL,** LearningDisability.com

Like Lynne and David, as you begin to implement the mindset and the mechanical how-to steps behind the *Multiple Streams* school of thought, your work as a coach will become immensely less constricting, and ultimately more rewarding.

I foresee that the number of coaches who will want to turn their backs on coaching will decline, and that the coaches who stick will increase their satisfaction to a level thus far unimagined.

As we discover financial success—and the new business models that support it—coaching will become a growth profession again, because it will once again be extraordinarily attractive.

Right now, it needs work! But we can do it.

Multiple Streams is about a long-term sustainable model of consistently making a difference in people's lives—on a large scale.

I call it "the new game of coaching," and I'm excited you're here.

Why I Wrote This Book

I have two purposes in writing this book.
First, to share with you what I now realize is the greater truth about what successful coaching looks like.

And second, to help you transform your relationship with coaching into a deep, an abiding, and—above all—a multifaceted one.

I've divided the book into several major sections.

I. In the first section, I talk generally about the shift from the old one-on-one model of coaching to the *Multiple Streams* approach. I talk about the convergence of coaching and internet marketing and how we can seize the opportunities it creates.

II. In the second section, I invite you to explore a unique coaching perspective of marketing. As I reframe some traditional perceptions of what marketing is, make sure your brain is loose and open. Shake out the curled up "roots" so they can breathe and absorb. This will let old ideas out and make room for new ones that will serve you better.

III. In the third section, I outline practical applications of the coaching approach to individual streams of income. In every stream, there are ways in which we can transfer the science and art of what we've learned to do one-on-one with clients, into information products, speaking engagements, and more. We'll be talking about the internet a great deal, as well as about the idea that you may want to get a job in order to become a better coach.

IV. In section four I address what to do when you wake up each morning and face the challenge of reorienting yourself to the new game of coaching. How do you get over the most common speed bumps? And how can you ease the transition from the old mindset to the new?

In short, keep reading to find out how to be in love with calling yourself a coach again—regardless of which streams of income you choose to major in at first.

Conversation Points

1. What formats are you currently using to coach clients?

2. How much are you enjoying your work and how many clients are you serving each month?

3. How much money are you currently making as a coach? Can you say, "I want to be a wealthy coach?"

4. Are you interested in learning new methods of delivering coaching? What benefit would you derive from doing so?

5. What is your vision for the impact of coaching on the world?

6. What do you hope your work in coaching will bring to you and to your family? What is your legacy?

The Demand for Coaching

The demand for coaching services has never been greater than it is today.

It's true.

Have you heard the saying, "Coaching is a solution that's looking for a problem?"

I'm here to remind you that as long as human beings are experiencing problems, there will always be a need for coaching.

It's just a question of stepping into the raging river of existing demand.

There's no need to artificially create a relentless demand for coaching. It already exists; the *trick* is to look at it with fresh eyes so you can see where it is—because it is NOT where most coaches are looking!

Never in the history of the coaching profession has this been truer—regardless of whose dates you use to count.

There are more coaches in the world today than ever before. Some say there are 40,000 coaches worldwide; others say half or double that number.

The fact is it doesn't matter.

You are a coach. Or you're wondering what being a coach is all about.

Either way, you want to earn a living, a good living. A lifetime of a living in fact.

Say it like it is, "I want to be wealthy."

And you are determined to do it by coaching, or it is doubtful you would have picked up this book.

Congratulations, it's a great dream and I deeply respect you for it.

Now are you ready to make it a reality?

Because if you are, it will take some work.

It will require some brutal honesty about your relationship with money.

But I'm here to tell you that actually tapping into the demand for coaching is quite straightforward.

Have you ever noticed that when you ask successful people what their secret is, it always ends up being something simple?

Ask an Olympic athlete, "What's your secret?"

The answer: Drink lots of water.

Ask the Dalai Lama, "What's most important?"

His answer: Focus on the breath.

Ask the best chefs in the world, "What matters most?"

The answer: The finest quality ingredients.

And ask a prima ballerina, "How did you dance so beautifully?"

COACHING IS A SOLUTION THAT'S LOOKING FOR A PROBLEM.

The answer: Practice, Practice, Practice.

AS LONG AS HUMAN BEINGS ARE EXPERIENCING PROBLEMS, THERE WILL BE A DEMAND FOR COACHING.

Every day, coaches drop out of the profession and turn their backs on what they thought was their dream. Every week, a coach comes to me to say, "Andrea, I think it's over. I can't make it as a coach."

This is horrible. And it doesn't need to be the case.

In fact, just the opposite. Hundreds of non-coaches are adding a 'coaching approach' to their current services and adding significant zeroes to their business bottom line!

You have to start by saying, "I want to do the great work of coaching AND I want to be wealthy."

If you've been sent to positively impact other people's lives, throwing in the towel is something I want you to avoid at all costs. Think about this, and when you feel ready to say, "I want to be wealthy," continue reading.

This book contains general marketing advice for new and veteran coaches alike, advice that's a consolidation of years of study, application and testing, in both online and offline worlds.

It contains descriptions and success stories of different streams of income that a coach can use to build wealth, using a coaching approach.

You'll find some of them unorthodox, such as Stream #10 *Get a Day Job*. If you are strapped for cash right now, and you cringe at the idea of cold calling or networking to try and get coaching clients, read *Get a Day Job* closely.

Some other streams you will have heard of, and perhaps you've even tried them, such as Stream #2, *Ecourses* or Stream #11, *Affiliate-based Promotions*, and many other streams that involve the online world. Now if you're saying to yourself, "Yeah, been there, tried that," stop. You need to know that each of the streams in this book has been selected carefully.

Why go to the trouble of writing a book for coaches and fill it will a bunch of hooey?

Every last stream of income in this book has been proven by your colleagues. Other coaches.

Now, it's just up to you whether you want to listen, learn and follow through on what's been proven to work.

Do you want to earn a wealthy income coaching?

Keep reading.

Conversation Points

Review why you are attracted to coaching. Is it because you are called? Is it because you enjoy learning new things? Is it because you enjoy having conversations with people? Are you running from something else?

Evaluate your level of motivation for doing the legwork required to succeed as a coach. Is it high or low? If it is high, how will you harness your energy and make rapid headway on the work ahead? If it is low, what daily practices can you implement that will get you in better shape? Meditation, prayer, exercise?

The Bigger Game is Really Big

It used to be that 100% of coaching occurred in one-on-one conversations.

The majority of the training and guidance for the profession has centered around that idea.

Perhaps that's because there is so much that's been borrowed or mirrored from the therapy model of doing business, who knows?

So much great coaching still does take place in that format. But the new game of coaching looks radically different.

It's much, much bigger than one-on-one conversations.

It's taking place in, and integrating itself into, the bigger marketplace in the form of many different formats and packages.

Coaching as a service is evolving into coaching as a product. Or a service/product hybrid. And that is a great big game that's exciting to behold.

In the bigger business world, this is a trend that pays to look at and listen to.

Why blur the lines between services and products? Because the market now demands it. As Mark Victor Hansen has said, "Everyone is now in the information marketing business."

Ford may be selling cars, but in a few years, look for them to be selling 'mobility services' instead.

How will you like buying a package that gives you a different vehicle to meet your different needs? A commuter car during the week, something gorgeous for that special occasion, a four wheel drive for the weekend and the camper for the summer?

'EVERYONE IS NOW IN THE INFORMATION MARKETING BUSINESS.'
- MARK VICTOR HANSEN

The fact is, it's the people with the guts and vision to realize now's the time to productize your services, or like Ford, 'service-ize' your product...who will lead the market by a mile.

So how do, you as a coach, productize what you have to offer? And in so doing, step into a much bigger game where you no longer trade time for money and you reach many hundreds and thousands of times more people with your important message?

To begin, commit to looking at your coaching as a solution to a specific problem.

So for example, instead of 'Time Management' as an offering, try

'How To Manage Your Overbooked Small Business and Get Your Life Back.'

See the difference?

Now frame this for a targeted group of people, and you go right to the top of the class.

'How to Manage Your Overbooked Plumbing Business and Get Your Life Back'

Or

'Time Management Tips To Increase Profits For the Busy Professional Plumber.'

Bingo, now that's a coaching product.

Continue by choosing a format or packaging option.

'How to Manage Your Overbooked Plumbing Business and Get Your Life Back in 6 Easy Chapters'

Or

'Listen to this 3-CD set, and learn how to manage your overbooked plumbing business and get your life back'

(You're welcome to run with this idea, by the way, and any others used as examples in the book. Just be sure to test the idea first, and when you're done send me a signed copy of your finished product so I can be the first to congratulate you.)

The siren call of the coaching industry has always been the dream that 'you can make lots of money helping others.' That by connecting with your passion to help others, you can make money.

And because for many coaches, it seems like you can't, many bright lights are leaving the coaching industry disillusioned, or worse, bitter.

The thing is you CAN make a living inspiring others.

But you must let go of the idea that coaching one-on-one - alone - is the way to do it.

Don't get me wrong, there are some truly wonderful coaches who are doing just that, and perhaps you are one of them.

The fact is, even the most successful one-on-one coach can leverage their abilities to achieve a better quality of life and evolve the human race too!

This leverage comes in the form of formats for delivering coaching which we are discussing. Many of these formats have unlimited capacity for reaching people and no time constraints.

Consider this: why should the world lose your gifts after you are dead?

You won't be able to coach one-on-one anymore, but your CD programs will live on, right?

One of the happiest moments for me recently came when coach

Chris Barrow floated this question:

> 'I want your opinion on something that is just an idea at this stage.
>
> I'm toying with the idea of turning The Dental Business School into a cookie cutter solution to apply to your chosen niche.
>
> The Chiropractors Business School.
>
> The Veterinarians Business School.
>
> You get it.
>
> A kind of franchise or licensing system.
>
> A relatively small number of clients, with my business earning an ongoing royalty based directly on their success (no win, no pay)'

Can you see how really very big this is? And how it takes the game to a whole new level of legacy building for Chris? It's perhaps his most important life work yet and is a perfect example of a Multiple Streams mentality.

Chris's idea
1. answers a specific problem,
2. targets itself towards a specific group of people, and
3. utilizes a tangible and recognizable format, franchise/licensing

These are truly exciting times for that area of the coaching world. If you aren't yet plugged in there, do so.

By choosing this book, and thoroughly investigating which of the

Multiple Streams of Coaching Income you will commit to building in the next 90 days, you too can take a step towards leaving a legacy of your work. One that will continue to coach thousands even after you're gone.

With thousands of coaches doing that, I see a future where every person on the planet will be exposed to coaching products of all sorts at every important juncture in their life.

It will truly become, 'A Coaching Solution for Every Problem.'

Now that's a vision worth looking at.

You can inspire for a living and earn a lifetime of wealth. Others in this book have.

For now, just savor the idea that the bigger game of coaching is really really big, much bigger than one-on-one coaching.
In fact, let me ask you this. To take advantage of the bigger game, are you ready to STOP coaching one-on-one?

Conversation Points

Fortune favors the bold. - Virgil, Aeneid

What is the biggest possible impact your coaching could have on the world? Even if it feels silly, talk about it openly with at least three people this week.

What specific problems will you solve with your coaching? (Examples: Lack of connection between busy parents and children. Single women who spend more money each month than they have earnings. Retired fashion models looking for a second career.) Make a list.

What The Buddha Says About Coaches

There is a Buddhist saying that goes like this:

If you meet the Buddha on the road, kill it.

This means to kill any concept of the Buddha as something apart from oneself.

To kill the Buddha is to BE the Buddha. Any concept we can have of the Buddha is so much smaller than the reality of what the Buddha actually is. And therefore any concept we have of the Buddha is limiting.

To experience the reality of the Buddha, we must destroy that concept in order to be free of the limitations.

Regardless of your spiritual beliefs, this analogy can be applied to coaches and coaching.

If you meet the Coach on the road, kill it.

This means to kill any concept of being a coach as something apart from oneself.

To kill the concept of coach is to BE a coach. To kill the coach means to throw away the idea that we can flick a switch and 'Be A Coach' while on the phone with a client, then hang up, and flick that switch off.

The philosophy behind Multiple Streams of Coaching Income is simple. Bring a coaching-rich approach to the creation of other streams of income, destroy our previous notions that being a coach means coaching one-on-one, and the result is:

• a much greater impact of coaching on the world
• a much greater means to earn wealth for coaches

If you've been coaching for a while, ask yourself, do you put on your role as a coach like a hat, and take it off after you hang up the phone with a client?

Do you have an ON/OFF switch that you flick, turning your role as coach on and off?

If yes, what would it be like for you to destroy your role as a coach and go beyond it?

 Conversation Points

How has being labeled a coach helped you? How has it hindered you?

Has the public responded well to the label of coach? Would it hurt your business somehow if you stopped calling yourself a coach?

What benefits can you imagine if you were to cast off the label coach?

Are You Ready To Stop Coaching One-on-One?

Let's put it simply, shall we?

As wonderful as it can be, one-on-one coaching alone simply won't support most coaches.

In combination with other coaching formats? Yes, that can do the trick very nicely.

As I started coaching half a dozen coaching clients in August 2003, I discovered quickly that business grew faster for the coaches who pursued other streams of coaching income in the early stages of their business building.

The ones who offered one-on-one coaching in combination with coaching products had a stronger and steadier flow of one-on-one coaching clientele than those who didn't.

In part, coaching products give you a credibility that attracts one-on-one clients.

But mostly, I know it's the business orientation a coach adopts when selling coaching products that helps the one-on-one business as a byproduct.

It also helps that you're not desperately grasping at clients because you have other means of financial support.

So whether you intend to coach one-on-one as 25% or 75% of your business pie, it's a smart move to take notes as you go through the book and identify which additional streams may be next for you.

Whichever you choose, bear in mind that you can design the new stream to generate revenue AND act as a referral engine for one-on-one clients, or, paying customers for your other products too.

Let me tell you the story of how I communicated this concept with a coaching client.

The client is a coach who'd had a full practice of 25 one-on-one clients for the previous year. By most measures she was doing very well indeed. And yet she was, by her own admission, absolutely miserable. And of course, that's why she was working with me as her coach.

She came to our sessions saying that she wanted to diversify her offerings and branch out more into internet marketing.

But did she really?

Quite quickly she seemed to get stuck. There was lots of resistance even though she said she wanted to act. And lots of flakiness when I would ask her if she'd like to look at what the resistance was about.

No problem, right? Big change takes time and courage, after all. So as her coach, I listened, continued to work on cosmetic type concerns at her request, supported and encouraged.

Until one day.

On that day I asked her why she loves coaching so much. We discussed her love of the profession for a few moments.

Then I asked her:

"Is your work as a coach important enough for you to STOP COACHING ONE-ON-ONE?"

There was silence.

More silence.

"I think so," she whispered at last.

Breakthrough.

Now here was a real opening for some progress in the direction of her dreams.

By stopping coaching one-on-one, you give yourself permission to leverage your time exponentially and reach thousands instead of dozens with your coaching message, using online marketing strategies and more.

With that shift, your goal of a coaching practice that comes with financial security AND ample time and freedom becomes doable.

So now it's your turn...

Are you putting all your coaching eggs in one basket?

Or as a small business coach once said to the fruit stand owner:

> You say you want to make more money, so stop putting everything in one basket. Don't just sell more apples. Bake some pies, make some jam, squeeze some cider. You'll make more money and along the way you'll sell more apples too.

 Conversation Points

How much time are you currently putting into marketing your one-on-one coaching services?

How can you divide the time you are currently investing into finding one-on-one clients into creating multiple streams of coaching income?

Why would multiple sources of coaching income be attractive to you in your particular situation?

X+Y+Z=Magic

Throughout this book you'll find a series of very special stories. As you find yourself lifted and inspired by the phenomenal impact that coaching is having in people's lives, I encourage you to ask yourself one question.

Are you interested in having that kind of impact?

A far-reaching, long lasting and highly leveraged impact. And at the same time, earning a lifetime of wealth for you and your family.

If your answer is, "Yes," terrific. Outlined below are the three steps you need to take to get started.

If your answer is, "Andrea, I don't know," I recommend that you in particular continue reading. And have a pad of paper and pen by your side to make some notes as you go along.

Or write directly into the margins of the book. I don't mind, it's what I do with every great book I read that really makes me think.

Whether you're a practicing coach, a small business owner, or a person looking to bring more abundance into your life, here is the simple three-step formula to creating new income streams:

NICHE + PROBLEM + FORMAT = ?

Figure 1: The Multiple Streams Formula

It's really as simple as that, but as they say, it's the simple steps that we as humans, for whatever reason, seem to want to skip.

We're ornery. Slippery. Stubborn. I doubt we'll ever get to the bottom of why that is, but it's the truth.

So let's give it a try.

Instead of skipping over this formula, take a moment and really consider it.

The temptation is strong, thinking there must be a magic pill somewhere else, something that will be easier than following these steps. Stop.

The success stories of coaches reaching hundreds and thousands of clients with 'AHA' moments are the proof. These coaches have tapped into the magic of this formula.

Exciting isn't it?

That could be you, if you're willing to take the formula seriously.

In fact, if your mission in life is to positively impact other people, you simply can't get around it. At some point, you'll have to stare this formula down or you'll just keep spinning your wheels.

Try adding the elements together and see:

1. Pick a niche market.

It could be acupuncturists, heart attack survivors, single dads, comic book collectors or organic food eaters.

Check out a fleshed-out list of niche markets in the Appendices. Circle or write down the ones that appeal to you. No need to select just one at this point.

It's enough that you start absorbing the fact that there is a niche market out there that is custom-fitted and waiting for you. And that by choosing one, you commit to changing lives within that niche.

2. Identify a specific problem that's occurring within that niche market.

Not enough time. Not enough customers. Too much stress. Symptoms of ill health. Boredom. Unfulfilled dreams. Stuck in a rut.

There is another list of universal problems that human beings experience in the Appendices. Once again, skim through, checking off or marking down the ones that catch your eye.

You'll narrow these down later. The exercise at this point is to get you to identify with a few very specific problems that your niche market is experiencing.

3. Choose a format to deliver your solution in.

A comprehensive list of formats is available in the Appendices to this book. Some of the major ones are of course showcased in the Table of Contents.

This is the packaging that your solution will come in. Just like sugar comes in packets, bags, cubes, sticks and even syrups; solutions come in all shapes and sizes.

To be the most effective at solving the problem you've selected within your niche market, you will eventually offer a full spectrum of packages.

For now, browse the Table of Contents for some packages that interest you the most.

Now, have some fun mixing them together.

For example, Nicola Cairncross, a coach who has reached more than 4,000 in her niche market in 9 countries around the world describes her formula as follows:

Niche?
- *Women 30-50*

PLUS

Problem?
- *Feeling out of control about money / Worry about financial future*

PLUS

Format?

- *10 Wealth Creation modules delivered by quarterly workshops covering four main lanes of the wealth highway*
- *One-to-one phone coaching to go deeper on individual circumstances*

EQUALS

- *New and sustainable income streams with many sub-products like teleclasses, eCourses, time management software, etc.*

Nicola is a sterling example of someone who has taken this very simple formula and run with it. Her six-going-on-seven figure coaching business is the proof.

To observe Nicola's modeling of the X+Y+Z=Magic formula first-hand, have a swing by her site at **www.nicolacairncross.com**

Conversation Points

What niche market do you belong in yourself? Perhaps you're a left-handed male, husband, father, grandfather, avid train collector who worked as a senior manager in the manufacturing industry and eats vegetarian. Whatever your characteristics are represent potential niche markets you may be here to serve. Make a list here, and add to it as new niches occur to you.

What problems do you encounter frequently? These may be problems you experience personally OR problems you help others solve. Are these problems you could help solve using a coaching approach?

Do you prefer working verbally or in writing? Do you enjoy talking or reading more? What kinds of personal development products do you purchase? These may be audio tapes, books, workshops, retreats, or all of the above. List them here as sign posts for types of packages you create for your clients.

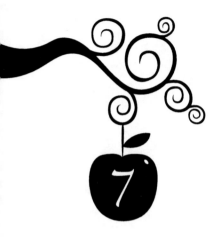

How Thomas Leonard Helped Most

One important thing I often reflected upon is that Thomas Leonard did very little one-on-one coaching in his lifetime.

It wasn't often remarked upon but it was a key characteristic of all the years he spent shaping the industry.

He was the ultimate coach's coach, and his coaching impacted hundreds of thousands of people for the better...but not through one-on-one coaching.

His directions were always clear: build the business to be flexible, systems-based and passive. His vision was definitely not limited by any notion of what a coaching practice ought to look like.

So what can you learn from Thomas' example?

You can look to what he built as an example of what you can do to change the world.

While he didn't label it as such, the business he spearheaded called

CoachVille was a textbook example of a coaching-rich, multiple streams business run with a die-hard coaching spirit.

Every month from September 2001 to August 2003, CoachVille used a tracking sheet in Microsoft Excel that outlined the performance of all streams of revenue and listed the new streams created that month.

For the health of the company, a target was set to create three to five new revenue streams per month.

And every line of the tracking sheet showed the number of units that had sold of each revenue stream in existence, whether that was the number of CoachVille members, the number of live event attendees, or the number of CD sets purchased.

This was the framework into which all the creative forces within CoachVille were poured, and as we worked the system, the results showed up in the form of massive growth each year.

IT'S TIME TO DESTROY WHAT WE'VE COME TO BELIEVE IS THE WAY TO DO COACHING.

Thomas was also a big one for destroying something in order to create something new.

The best example of this was when we agreed it was time to make membership in CoachVille free.

Previously priced at $79 for a lifetime membership, CoachVille grew to more than 25,000 members over the course of two and a half years. It had been, shall we say, a rather healthy revenue stream. Now, we decided to make membership free.

The result of this act of creative destructionism was something bigger and better which more than made up for that stream of revenue. But, that doesn't mean it didn't take courage to take that step and destroy our old model.

Nature does the same thing doesn't it? Tornados, forest fires, and even earthquakes, although causes of great devastation, also create something vigorous and new in their wake, given time.

Thomas' acts of creative destructionism as a businessperson are also great lessons to us as we look into the future of coaching.

Could it be that it's time to creatively destroy the one-on-one model of coaching? I think it is.

I think it's time to destroy what we've come to believe is 'the way to do coaching'. And time to make room for a new way to bring coaching to the world.

It's time to bottle it. Time to build bottling factories, distribution channels, transportation systems and bottle stores, thousands of them, all over the world.

Welcome to the new game of coaching where you can learn how. It's not as fearsome as it might seem. In fact, it's called Multiple Streams of Coaching Income and over 1000 of your coaching colleagues are bottling away as we speak.

So even if you don't understand distribution channels or transportation systems, it's okay, that's why you're reading this book.

All will become clear, I promise.

Conversation Points

What do you think of the idea of destroying the one-on-one model of coaching as the primary method coaching gets delivered?

What innovative ways can coaching be delivered that have not yet been imagined?

What are your next steps towards making them a reality?

Convergence

Psst....you there, reading this book. Yeah. Quiet for a second.

Do you hear that?

That hush.

Like someone holding their breath.

You know that sound. It's the sound before something big happens.

Here's the thing. As a student of history, sociology and anthropology, I've observed that big things happen when two or more previously separate worlds touch, or as they sometimes do, collide.

Big breakthroughs occur, inventions burst out, sometimes there's serious conflict.

It's the same way weather happens – when heat and cold meet, you get X. When high pressure meets low pressure, you get Y.

The convergence of internet marketing and direct marketing with the coaching profession is going to be just like that. Some spectacular weather is getting ready to happen.

And for you who are ready for it, there's plenty of rainmaking on its way.

Think of it in terms of a Venn Diagram:

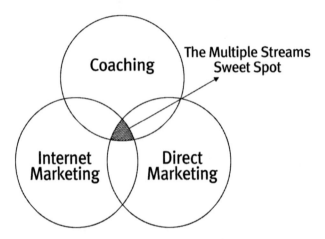

Figure 2: The Convergence of Internet Marketing, Direct Marketing and Coaching

Internet marketing using a coaching approach has a great hey-day ahead of it.

And coaching, with its reach amplified and its impact deepened by using internet and direct marketing tools, also has massive things waiting for it.

It's just a matter of who will step in and harness a part of that energetic wave for their benefit. I'm making it my business to do so in a way that helps thousands of coaches. Will you join in?

Oh by the way. The internet is about to go through some big

changes now too. It's headed for some terrific convergence with direct marketing techniques.

Just imagine if we put together the power of the internet to collect leads with powerfully proven direct marketing techniques to convert those leads to sales? Whew, that is on the verge of quite a little gold rush.

It's already starting to happen, albeit quietly for the moment. But watch for it. When this breaks out, great things – multiple, manifold fortunes - are anticipated. All as a result of the integration of offline and online marketing techniques.

In fact, those fortunes are amassing now.

Within this context, what the Multiple Streams of Coaching Income approach can do is help you see the coming changes through the lens of a coach, and help you sort out what this means for you and your livelihood.

Conversation Points

Have you noticed internet marketers adding 'coaching programs' to their offerings of late? In what way could your coaching business benefit by adding 'internet marketing' to the mix?

How are you as a coach uniquely suited to using online strategies to build your business? (Hint, it has to do with what makes a great coach.)

When it comes to new opportunities for business, do you consider yourself an early-adopter? Why or why not?

A great marketing book on this topic is *Marketing Convergence: How the Leading Companies Are Profiting from Integrating Online and Offline Marketing Strategies* by Susan K. Jones. Want to leapfrog to the front of the line on this? Read it.

Marketing

If you don't like the way something looks, change the way you look at it.

—Wayne Dyer

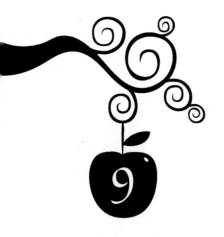

The Great Marketing Reframe

I don't know how many times I've gone off on a rant about marketing.

With people I work with of course, (I don't know if Kerri has ever recovered), in my bloggings, and even, yes, this is dire, with my husband Mike.

Mike was one of these people for whom marketing had always been a bad word. It represented an invasion, an affront, all things that disgust.

And while I'm not saying he's 180 degrees from that now, I know our debates have mellowed a lot. (Or maybe he's just letting me think that, dear man.)

When it comes to discussing marketing with coaches, it's much the same thing. From grimaces to stomach knots, talking about marketing seems to take on the sound of Charlie Brown's teacher, with so many syllables of, "*wah WAaah, wah WAah, wah.*"

What does this mean?

For starters, I find it terrifyingly ironic that, when it boils down to it, truly - marketing and coaching are actually ONE.

Yes that's right. I may be in the minority, but it's served me very well to see marketing and coaching with an equal sign between them...as in, they are equivalent.

At its heart, coaching is nothing but an advanced level of communicating, or as some might prefer, relating. Great coaching expands your awareness, lights a fire under you, and makes you shout, "Eureka!"
In the same way, great marketing is really just communication.

It causes action.

Coaching AND marketing both, when they're doing their 'thing'... bridge gaps of understanding. They solve problems.

But of course when great marketing is being done on behalf of things, people or concepts that we don't like or agree with (politicians, warfare, annoying television, anything being marketed at the dinner hour) THEN of course, we begin to hate marketers and marketing.

An aside, I really think the way to get over this angst around marketing is to let ourselves be convinced or not convinced, whatever way the message is being delivered, AND whether we are convinced or not, reserve the right to NOT buy.

A lot of the reason why people (coaches too) feel the need to be rude to a telemarketer is because they're afraid of being sold, and spending money they don't have.

We seem to think that once we are convinced we have no other recourse than to buy.

No.

It's more like this:

Oh yes, that is a wonderful discount. Yes, that was a delicious sample, thank you. I agree it will be sad if I miss this chance. It would be nice. And thank you anyway. I have quite a few possessions, e-books, CDs, training materials, and souvenirs that I haven't fully enjoyed yet, so I'll be doing that instead.

But I digress.

COACHING AND MARKETING ARE ONE AND THE SAME

As you read through this book and engage with the paradigm shifts within, I invite you to consider that every time you think about the activity called marketing...you substitute the word coaching.

When you think about writing a sales letter for your website, call it a coaching letter instead. Your goal is to coach that person to the right decision for them about this product of yours.

You might say, *"But Andrea, coaching is a two-way thing where I do a lot of listening before responding, writing a sales letter is me at my desk all alone..."*

Yes! It's true. And that's why a good sales letter cannot be written in a vacuum. A great sales letter is always a representation of the market research or listening you've done before you created your product.

So if you've followed the Multiple Streams formula, you've asked your market what they most need and want at this time.

That's the listening part.

You then boiled that down and created a product based on what you've heard.

That's the responding or coaching part.

Does that make sense?

Yes it's a reframe, and probably a significant one for many.

What if your marketing letter falls flat and you're not making any sales?

That means one of three things:

1. You haven't listened well in the first place.
2. The words you've chosen aren't the right words.
3. The style in which you're writing the words isn't connecting with your readers.

Now reread those three things and tell me if those aren't three major reasons why coaching also falls flat.

So try it, whenever you think about doing something dreaded like 'marketing' of any kind, think of it as coaching instead. Draw

from your deep well of conviction and passion that you are here to coach. Then, do your marketing.
Be sure to write and tell me how it goes.

I've lived with this idea for a few years now and it holds water very well.

One of the biggest things I've learned in the past several years is how to write in a coaching manner. How to present information in a way that engaged.

I must tell you that there was a LOT of bumps along that road.

The reason I share this story with you is this. When I finally got it, I realized, all I have to do is write in the same way as I coach.

The line between coaching and marketing is a silk gossamer thread; there really is no line.

Coach-like writing IS hard at first.
Practice it by copying proven marketing text by hand. It's a tip the top-grossing copywriters use and it works.

I can vouch for it. Keep practicing and you will get better at communicating in a coach-like way in your writing...and creating dynamite marketing copy by doing so.

Beyond that, I'll be the first person to tell you that marketing copy is only successful if it brings in sales. So the first and only rule of thumb when you go to write marketing (coaching!) material is to test, test, test...and keep the version that sells most.

That's it!

The fact is I'm waiting for a humungous 'aha' on this.

I've coached a few internet marketers now on the benefit of adopting a coaching approach. It's a funny thing, maybe a bit like coaching an accountant to relax and round everything to the dollar.

But for those that are open enough to this coaching wind up understanding. The idea that marketing really is coaching has brought their sales to a whole new level. That's because the depth of connection with their markets has increased dramatically.

As coaches, that's pretty much a 'shrug' right? "*Well yeah, Andrea, that's what's so cool about coaching. When people get 'coaching' their life changes.*"

But that's not the bigger 'aha' I'm waiting for.

I'm waiting for coaches to get that while all the internet marketers out there still have to learn what coaching is, there is a huge opportunity for coaches.

It's one thing to have the heart of a coach and learn the techniques of marketing. You can become a member in Multiple Streams of Coaching Income for that!

It's a whole other ball game to be a die-hard salesperson or internet marketer and not have any idea that a thing called 'coaching' can help increase revenue.

So what are we waiting for, coaches?

Like I said to Kerri in that unexpected hour-long rant about marketing.

All marketing is communication.

If you have ever suffered the pain of not being able to communicate something, be it in the middle of heated debate, or in the face of a language barrier, you know the pain of not being able to sell something.

If you have ever felt misunderstood, based on how you look, your size, shape, color or demeanor, you've experienced a marketing problem.

How you dress is marketing, your posture is marketing, the state of your lawn is marketing. The paper your resume is on is marketing. In New York and every other city in the world, the location of your office is absolutely marketing.

What are you communicating about yourself as a coach? How is that equivalent to how you are marketing your business as a coach?

If you are ready to try on the mindset that all marketing is a form of coaching, what can you now release yourself to do with ease, pleasure and even...passionate abandon?

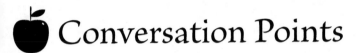 Conversation Points

What are three things about marketing that you have resisted doing or learning? In what way are these things in fact coaching, under a different name? Does this help you get these things done?

In the last 30 days, what piece of marketing did you respond to well as a consumer? A television commercial? A radio advertisement? A brochure in the mail? How can you emulate that piece of marketing for an aspect of your business?

There's That Word 'Niche' Again

In a single day, the average adult uses more than 35,000 words.

That's a lot of talking.

To illustrate something here, take a moment and multiply 35,000 by the number of people in your household. And then multiply it by the number of people you GUESS are within a 10-mile radius of where you sit right now.

A guess is fine.

That's a LOT of words, isn't it?

JUST WHO DO YOU THINK IS LISTENING?

Now multiply by the number of people on the internet, and then, why not, do it just one more time by the population of the world.

Now let me ask you a question.

With all that talking, just who do we think is listening?

There are a lot of definitions of the word niche. The most generic one is two words:

Target Market

What is a target market? For our purposes, it's a group of people who have common interests and problems. Coaches of course, are ourselves a niche.

Solo business people, some say, are quite a large niche, and one with great possibilities.

Mystery writers are a niche. So are Siamese cat owners, real estate agents, Americans living abroad, lactose intolerant children and parents of twins.
Lately, the word niche has been popping up a lot.

And if I continue to have my way, you'll keep hearing it.

Because as we established in the previous chapter, if all marketing is simply communication, then NOT choosing a target market is like trying to get your voice heard by the rest of the world over the din of all those other people talking.

In fact, it would be very similar to you putting down this book right now, going out to your front yard and yelling at the top of your lungs that you have a fantastic teleseminar going on next week.

You just aren't going to be heard.

At a crowded party, if I'm interested in communicating something to someone, I need to locate that person, get to within speaking distance of him, and then say something that he's interested in hearing.

The context of the example makes it simpler to understand, right?

There's no point saying, "Want to go somewhere where it's quieter?" from the other side of the bar. That just isn't logical.

Now whereas it's been 10 years now since I thoroughly and contentedly left the singles scene, this is an example that makes sense to most everyone.

If you want to communicate something to someone, whether it's to get them to do something, think something, feel something or believe something, you need to know who you want to communicate that thing to.
And that's the essence behind the exercise of choosing a niche market.

No one can market to everyone; it's just too expensive, even for big players like Coca-Cola or Pepsi.

In fact, both of those companies spend a lot of time breaking down their market into segments. There's a whole different language and even different colors and sounds they employ to market to teenagers, as compared to adults who've been drinking the product for decades.

For a coach, whether you're a solopreneur or work for a coaching company, the clearer you are about your target market, and the more passionate you are about it, in fact, the more likely your streams of revenue are going to grow...quickly and dramatically. Now I have a pet theory when it comes to coaches and choosing niche markets, and it's one that some people may not want to hear.

I'm not talking about if you haven't figured out which market you want to work with yet. There are lots of good reasons for that. Most of us just haven't been wired to do this and it takes some shifting to get there.

It's the person who hears all about the massive benefits of choosing a niche, and then turns around and actively ignores that information. It's still astonishes me that they blithely go on their way continuing to market to the world.

This in my opinion is a complete act of hubris. Harmless, but still hubris. It's a kind of unintentional ego trip.

Coaches who cater more to their own desire to help the world instead of actually helping a segment of it, really aren't in it for anyone but themselves and their feeling of making a difference.

It's sad, but 100% the truth. Think about it.

Not very many people know that one of the business strategies I'd lobbied for at CoachVille was to niche-market coach training.

What's that?

For the owners of coach-training organizations reading this, it's your turn to sit up.

This was a strategy to activate a long list of new domain names. It was a themed group of domains, all intended to introduce the benefits of studying and using a coaching approach to various professions.

- CoachingForRealtors.com
- CoachTrainingForRealtors.com
- CoachingForAttorneys.com (This one is being utilized nicely and well by Coach Daniel Roberts, good to see.)
- CoachingForPoliticians.com
- Etc.

Initial testing of these markets showed responsiveness to being trained in the tenets of coaching.

In particular, realtors saw the benefit of taking a coaching approach when working with buyers who (1) don't know what kind of house they want (2) can't make a joint decision with their spouse or even (3) can't understand why they shouldn't be working with more than one agent.

And that's just one example.

So if you're a coach training organization, have at it!

For the rest of you, let this be another example of how niche marketing can help, especially in an industry where there is a lot of competition, like coach training.

Back to the importance of niche marketing for the individual coach, like you and I.

The fact is you just can't market to everyone. But because coaches wouldn't be coaches if we weren't so passionate about doing good, it's a thorny challenge to get a coach to say "yes" to a certain niche market because...

Sooner or later they figure out that it means you have to say no to the rest of the world.

One of my one-on-one clients illustrates it best. She told me she had done some research and narrowed her market down. To which I said, of course, "*Terrific.*"

"*I've decided to work ONLY with women.*"

Needless to say there was a bit of a silence on my end of the telephone, followed by a smile. "*Can you hear me smiling at you?*" said the Coach to the Client.

Sigh.

I understand. I really do. In working with my own coach, I'm very clear that my gift is giving people around me the love and courage they need to do absolutely anything.

When people get around me, if they hang around for a while, they get great.
And so as a coach, of course I'm eager to share that.

But then, there came a dark moment: "Oh. I can't do that for the world."

So I've committed to communicating my gifts to the very special group of people called coaches.

I've been blessed to be able to see things strategically for coaches. All of you who write to me saying, "*Is the dream dead, I just can't make any money*", continue to validate my decision and I thank you.

Here's the thing here. It's a greater truth about choosing a niche market that I've discovered in one-on-one practice.

Choosing a niche market is a lot like figuring out your purpose in life. Many of us have, I'm sure, worked with clients to answer the question, "*What's my mission in life?*"

And as we all know, this question is often a stumper.

There are more than a hundred books and probably as many programs, tapes, and twice again the number of motivational speakers who talk all about finding our mission in life.

Don't get me wrong, I'm not disparaging this. It's just that at a certain point, trying to find one's mission starts to feel a lot like pushing string.

For some of you choosing a niche market may feel a lot the same.

Let me say this. If you find it hard to choose a niche, that's okay. Do the exercises at the end of the chapter, and continue to walk the road, holding the intention and the understanding that there is a group of people with common interests and problems, that YOU are here to serve.

You and the sum of your knowledge, experience, skills and wisdom are a gift to that group of people, in a way that's just like peas are meant for carrots.

At the same time, pay special attention to Income Stream #11 later in the book, about building a coaching revenue stream using Affiliate Programs. This gives you a way to get on the Multiple Streams path while you're still figuring it out.

While you're doing that, one day your niche will jump out and bite you where you sit up and notice.

A reminder. This finding a niche thing is similar to discovering your mission in life in more than one respect. It's not something you can find using only your brain.

As the author Richard Bolles said in his book What Color Is Your Parachute?, "Your mission is where the world's deepest hunger and your heart's greatest gladness intersect." And the same goes for your niche.

> RICHARD BOLLES SAID, "YOUR MISSION IS WHERE THE WORLD'S DEEPEST HUNGER AND YOUR HEART'S GREATEST GLADNESS INTERSECT."
>
> THE SAME GOES FOR YOUR NICHE.

Just don't try to force-think your way to an answer. Continue on and make the mental shifts set out in this book. Chop wood and carry water, put one foot in front of the other. Test. Experiment. Play.

Once your mind has been stretched to accommodate new ideas or questions such as, "What is my niche market?" it will never go back to its old shape.

Listen carefully. Your niche is out there, and once found, it will coach YOU to be a better coach.

Ain't personal growth grand?

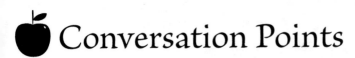 Conversation Points

Here is a great exercise based loosely in parts on Jay Abraham's work in *Your Secret Wealth*.

Note 1: Many of you may have already gone through exercises like this one. Go ahead and do it again. Be conscious of not using only your mind to answer, especially this time. The other times you may have used your brain to come up with results. Try writing from your heart.

Note 2: As you proceed, remember that you are already living your mission on some level. Begin where you are now.

We all want to believe that we are unique, and here for a special reason. It's just human nature and we all have it. What inkling do you have about why you in particular, are here?

The truth is that there will never be anyone exactly like you in the world. Who are you a gift for? Who is waiting for you to arrive exactly as you are right now?

Take a moment to review your previous coaching clients.

Describe each of them thoroughly and make note of any common threads. What profession was your most enjoyable client? What characteristic of client do you tend to attract? What similar problems do your clients seem to have?

List your previous jobs or businesses. What business were you in? What customers did you serve? If it's been awhile, dust off your most recent resume and read between the lines for new insights.

Often, people who feel on the cusp of having a breakthrough insight into their purpose, or the niche market they're uniquely suited to serve, find that a simple series of questions can push them over the edge into realization.

Is your mission actually a lot bigger than what you are imagining? Or maybe it's smaller (and less ponderously important seeming) than what's in your mind's eye?

Is the niche market you are considering actually bigger than what you have thought of so far? Or maybe it's quite a bit smaller and less intimidating?

If it weren't important to have a niche market, what would you do with yourself to earn a living with your coaching business this year?

Document the Knowledge, Experience and Skills that you've collected. Free associate. Write down what you think of first. Repeat.

1. Knowledge, Experience or Skill

How have you utilized this in your work to date? How have you underutilized it?

Exercise:

Go to one or all of these locations on the internet, and browse the categories of people who have gathered to share common interests and problems.

List the group names, online communities, forums, discussion lists and chat groups that pique your interest.

Yahoo Groups – www.YahooGroups.com
Google Groups – www.GoogleGroups.com
Dmoz – www.Dmoz.com
About – www.About.com

Sign up for a handful of the ones that you are most interested in, and to save you time later, bookmark them while you are there.

When you've worked through the exercises for this chapter, review your answers and see what groups of people stick out, and create a shortlist. This may become a working list of possible niche markets you can serve.

Continue to work this path with other Multiple Streamers by phone or in groups near you. It will set you on a good steady pace along the path to building your multiple streams of coaching income, and make you a better coach too.

Oh and yes, it goes without saying -- do tap into the wisdom of your own coach. I'm sure they'll be delighted.

Okay, But Where Is the Money, Really?

Over the course of hearing from hundreds of coaches this year, this is the question that comes up most.

"Andrea, where do all the successful coaches hang out? And what kinds of business models are they using?"

Love these questions.

And the answer in brief is this chapter.

First, it's true that coaches on the whole don't have a habit of talking about success. That's part of the dialog I hope to see change as you digest and create conversations around the concepts in this book.

Many people talk about the importance of empirical evidence to support the benefits of coaching. I think talking about our successes is a gateway to that kind of cold, hard proof.

A quick aside.

If you'd like to spearhead the project of collecting fact-based before and after coaching success stories, get in touch with me right away.

Envision 100 compelling 'Life Makeover' stories that bring the media's attention in a way that is based on results.

I'll be more than happy to submit my story as a coaching client of multiple first-rate coaches to get it started and I will enlist the help of every Multiple Streams reader.

Let's change this strange habit of cloaking our results in mystique in the name of confidentiality.

Although we may not be able to share our clients' successes, we can certainly share our own breakthroughs.

Now as far as what kinds of business models are working, excellent question. Here it is.

There is a universal model that Multiple Streams coaches have used, and will continue to use for a long time to come, and it's in the form of a funnel.

Many online entrepreneurs don't even realize they are using this business model, but if you look hard enough, you should be able to see it in the infrastructure.

Also, as of this writing there is a twist to the funnel model that I will share. I hope you pay attention to this twist because from what I can see, it has fantastic potential. By the time this book is in your hands, I'll be testing it on my own site so you can stay tuned for more.

But more on that a little later.

Introducing the Multiple Streams Ice Cream Journey

As you'll have noted by now, I'm a big believer in metaphors. Especially when we're breaking down old paradigms, comparing something that seems taken for granted to something else unexpected can have a great mind-expanding effect.

I like to describe the Multiple Streams Business Model in terms of Ice Cream. Here is what I mean.

Figure 3: Multiple Streams Ice Cream Journey

If you've ever been to an Ice Cream Store, you very likely have asked to try a flavor before you decide what to get. In some cases, they give you the taste on a very small pink spoon.

Maybe you don't like the first flavor your try. So you ask for another pink spoon. And probably within a couple of tries, you decide on what you'd like. And you order an ice cream cone of that flavor.

Now, if you're anything like me, after awhile you stop ordering ice cream cones, and instead take home a small pint of your favorite flavor so you can have it anytime.

And of course, maybe on a special occasion, I might order an ice cream cake in that flavor too...I've started to really become attached to it, you see.

Now it's true that somewhere along the line I may get tired of one flavor and go back to the beginning, and try a few more. That's what's so great about those little pink spoons, if you ask me!

On the other hand, I have a friend who's a particular fan of ice cream, and she's become a member of a 'Flavor of the Month Club' and gets regular deliveries of the specialty flavor to her door, once a month.

Interesting, isn't it?

As you consider this Ice Cream Journey of business, I invite you to review Figure 3 on the previous page. It shows the Ice Cream Journey in the shape of a Funnel.

The Pink Spoon is above the widest part of the Funnel. The Ice Cream Cone is next. The pint-sized containers are next again, and the bottom of the funnel is filled out with an Ice Cream Cake and the Ice Cream Flavor of the Month Club.

On the next few pages we'll talk more specifically about how successful Coaches have used the Ice Cream Model to construct very viable and sustainable businesses based on these principles.

For now though, let me pin down just a few simple observations:

1. The more people who try the Pink Spoon at the top of the funnel, the more will likely go ahead and purchase an ice cream cone. The more people who enjoy an ice cream cone, the more likely they are to purchase a pint of ice cream. And so on down the funnel.

It all starts with a free taste, however, the proverbial Pink Spoon.

2. As the customer travels down the funnel, many things are happening. They are building a relationship with the company. They are gradually spending more money.

And yes, some people are proceeding to a certain level in the funnel and then stopping.

3. Many coaches already offer the equivalent of a Pink Spoon. Think for a moment, of what yours might be. If you said 'a free coaching session,' you definitely aren't alone.

Although it works to a degree, giving away a free coaching session is like giving away not a Pink Spoon taster but a giant bowl of Ice Cream, for no charge.

So one of the first things the Multiple Streams Product Funnel will coach you to do is refine your Pink Spoon so it truly is a taste, and doesn't give away the store.

Still more coaches, in following the one-on-one coaching model, try to build their businesses with Pink Spoons and Flavor of the Month Clubs only. They spend the majority of their effort trading time for money at the very 'bottom' of this funnel... unnecessarily frustrated. This is what we call a 'too hot' funnel. A 'just right' funnel spreads your energy (active & passive) - and cultivates results and impact - smoothly through the layers.

Remember: The product funnel model is based on real-world success, NOT theory.

The Ice Cream Journey is a fantastic mental model to help you plan a step-by-step journey for your potential clients to take.

Now...having said all this, I think you can start to see the power behind the metaphor. Would you like to start talking about how to transfer the learning points from the metaphorical Ice Cream Journey to your Multiple Streams Coaching Business? Read on.

The Traditional Product Funnel Blueprint

Figure 4: The Traditional Product Funnel

This is the Multiple Streams Product Funnel, and as you can see, this example has five bands or tiers, much like the Ice Cream Funnel we covered earlier.

As you progress to the bottom of the funnel, the price point of the product or service increases.

Accordingly, it's safe to say that as you build your own version of this funnel, you'll concentrate your most valuable material, put it in the market's most desired packaging, and position the resulting offering at the bottom of the funnel. Because that's the position that fetches the highest price.

Let's go over the first band in a bit more detail.

As you can see from the diagram, the top-most band is the complimentary offering or Pink Spoon.

This is an information product you offer to the market to give them the opportunity to get to know you, without having to pay you money.

Most often, the free offering is a mini-e-book, a newsletter, mini-course, or special report.

If you are getting set to create your first free offering, I recommend you choose a finite item rather than a newsletter. If you choose a newsletter, make sure you have the drive to sustain it.

Writing a weekly or even monthly newsletter can really freeze some coaches up, especially those who aren't writers. Although do remember that there's plenty of room for an audio newsletter...

Whatever format you use, try not to lock yourself into a fixed publication schedule. Instead, commit to publishing at least twice a month but only when something of significance that's of great use to your readers comes up.

They'll appreciate your discretion more than your regularity.

Once you've created your free offering, give it to readers who agree to share their email address as a thank you for their permission to create an ongoing dialog.

With this gift of their permission, you now have the opportunity to offer valuable information and develop some unparalleled relationships of trust.

Entrepreneurs who haven't worked in the online medium have expressed their amazement at how intimate a relationship can form using this method. In their eyes, it's pure heaven, because of course intimacy and trust means a rock solid bond with the client. I say this simply because it bears remembering for those of us who can tend to take email marketing for granted.

Later when you have offerings that may interest your readers, you can then introduce them in the course of your publication. In online marketing, this is the process that, for the most part, leads to the bulk of sales.

Now each price level in the model above will naturally flow into the next, and as your clients follow your work, you'll find a growing group that continues to buy your new offerings. As you get to know your market, your offerings will reflect more and more strongly their real needs, and your client satisfaction goes through the roof.

And that, simply put, is what creates lifelong coach-client relationships that will sustain your business.

An increasing number of coaches, not to mention internet marketers as well, of course, are making a respectable living using a model as simple as the above.

It may look simplistic, but with elbow grease, it works very well, usually to the tune of six figures per annum depending on the niche market you picked.

Remember the Multiple Stream formula?

Niche + Problem + Packaging = Coaching Income

The ezine in this case is the grease on the skids that makes this formula possible.

If you are persistent, do the sometimes dusty work to continue to build the readership of your free offering, and innovate the offerings in your marketing funnel frequently, you can follow in the footsteps of coaches who have made it work for up to five or more years.

It does take determination however.

Now here's the twist.

The Product Funnel example above hinges on conversion. How many people visit your website? Of those, how many signed up for your free ezine? That's one important statistic.

Of the people who signed up for your ezine, how many people

bought your first-tier product? Another conversion statistic.

And so on, down the bands of the Product Funnel.

In fact, in some internet marketing circles, the saying goes, "*There are only two things you need to know how to do to make money online. Get traffic. And convert traffic.*"

The twist is this. It's now being proven that it's better to stop collecting subscribers for your free ezine. That it's much much better to collect the email addresses of people who will pay for shipping and handling for a free CD.

Have a look at this link from Brian Tracy's site for example:

www.briantracy.com/21ss/smm/

This illustrates the twist to the traditional model in full-color.

In exchange for your email address and $4.95 in shipping and handling, Brian Tracy will send you a CD or audiocassette.

The many hundreds of people who accept his offer each month become part of a valuable database of leads who have demonstrated their willingness to spend money.

In comparison with a subscriber who has spent no money to receive an ezine, the 'money lead' in the previous example is much more likely to purchase something at the next level of the funnel.

The conversion rates are much higher.

Of course, because you are shipping the CD or audiocassette at a small loss to you, it's important that you are ready with other products in the Product Funnel to present and recommend to your newly collected money leads.

Here's how the Product Funnel looks with a twist:

Figure 5: The "Twisted" Product Funnel

It's an exciting opportunity I'll be putting into place, so stay tuned at the Multiple Streams of Coaching Income site. I'll report the results to you as they come in.

So now that you know the business model, let's get even more detailed.

You asked, "Where is the money?"

Below are three real permutations of the above model.

In each case they are real businesses that have built these models over time. Each has been in operation for six months or more.

Example #1:

- free newsletter
- free sample teleseminars
- free mini-ebook
- free resource lists and forms
- free graphical logos

- $15+ gift items such as key chains, t-shirts, etc.

- $39 advertising in newsletter
- $39 CDs/Tapes

- $79 lifetime membership
- $99 six-week teleseminar programs
- $99 multi-part eCourses

- $179 two-day live events
- $99, $199 or $299/month high-end membership

- $5000 high-end licenses

Given a very active niche market and a very active team behind the creation of products for this organization, this model grew rapidly to millions of dollars in gross revenue.

Example #2:

- free newsletter
- free intro teleseminars
- free audio samples

- $179 and $229 two-day live events

- $179 recorded live event

- $450/monthly coaching membership

With an emphasis on value, credibility and a very strong knowledge of the niche market, this business took this model and broke the six-figure mark within 30 days of launch.

Example #3:

- free newsletter
- free intro teleclasses
- free mini-ebook

- $25 print book
- $37 per month beginner level membership
- $47 multi-part eCourse

- $77 one-time teleseminars
- $129 CD set
- $129 one-day live training

- $279 big box product

- $500 per month one-on-one coaching
- $1050 per month one-on-one coaching

- $995 two-day intensive boot camps
- % revenue share consulting projects

With an emphasis on monthly subscription services and cash flow, I have been particularly happy with my Product Funnel, shown in this example.

This is now the foundation of a six-figure business I've been running on about 30 hours of work per week.

Suffice to say that the model holds up to a great deal of variation but the fundamentals are important.

You have a great deal of leeway and flexibility to fashion your own version of the Product Funnel for multiple streams of income.

✓ A lot depends on your positioning statement, and how strongly you bond with your market especially in your gift offering. More on positioning in a later chapter.

If you're looking to walk the shortest path to money, focus the majority of your energy on the first paying level in your product funnel.
Make sure you spend some time ascertaining what the market wants most from you at this time. And then deliver exactly what it wants.

But let me talk for a moment about the bigger picture.

There is a bit of a point I want to make about money and coaches.

To so many people, perhaps including you, money is a dirty word. It's something there isn't enough of, or it's too hard to get, or it represents evil. Really! If you don't have preconceived negativity towards money, be sure to say a special thank you for that to whoever brought you up.

For the majority who do have baggage around money, this is something worth getting over, not just for you, but for your clients too. Coaches have hearts that beat so strongly for doing good in this world; money mostly takes a back seat.

The fact is, there are great livings to be earned through coaching, and the coaches in the Multiple Streams membership are proving it.

So what is the bottom line?

Money is simply a symbol of value.

Wealthy people are proof that when you create real value for someone else or better yet many someone else's, money cannot help but follow.

The more value you create, the more money follows. If you aren't earning any money as a coach, could it be that you aren't - YET - creating a significant value proposition that attracts clients?

Just like shells, cows, camels, silks or smiles, you can measure the value you trade with dollars, yen and rupees. Ask yourself, does your coaching prowess, in whatever format, deserve to be sold?

Is it valuable?

There are people in this world who can only hear what you have to say, from you.

Do they deserve to receive your message in exchange for their dollars?

Whatever you do, keep working on your relationship with money. It has deep roots.

For me, I know that along the path to an enlightened relationship with money, it's helped me to practice the art of gracious receiving.

As my coach says, *"Do you know those people, Andrea, who when they go to their friend's house, or to a party, always have to bring something? Like a friend, a bottle of wine or a dessert?"*

These people find it very hard to show up as themselves, without bringing something 'with.' On their own, they aren't valuable enough to show up, so they have to bring a bonus.

They don't believe that they are enough just as they are. And it's the same for us.

It used be a hot topic to talk about taking time for ourselves, to enjoy a massage, and practice self-care. Now I think we're ready to practice extreme **self-wealth**.

By receiving wealth, we free ourselves to give even more, and the circle continues.

Now pick up your pen and start building some Product Funnel examples that work for you. There's space at the end of the chapter.

If money flows back and forth in a loop, who are you to be blocking up the whole system?

Get up, get out, and get earning money. It all starts with your answers to the questions in this book.

Conversation Points

What would you like your Product Funnel to look like? Draw several upside-down triangles below and fill them in. You can include the products you already offer, if any, then start filling in the gaps with possible products.

More about the different packaging options follows in the book, but for now, sketch out a few possible funnels. You'll come back to this exercise and refine it as your knowledge of what fits for you expands.

In my experience, those of us who can identify a greater reason to unashamedly and enthusiastically earn money have an easier time of it.

In keeping with this, it can be useful to identify a greater goal for money. It was a special moment when I created a revenue stream dedicated to a worthy cause.

That's one of the greatest feelings about mastering online marketing and the various streams of income. You then have the ability to give the gift of a revenue stream to others. You can turn on new revenue streams on behalf of others.

At an internet-marketing seminar, I listened with mixed feelings, but was impressed at the same time, when I heard the speaker talk about what he calls his 'BMW product.' It's an e-book that he created to cover his new BMW payments, which it does nicely, bringing in about $500 per month.

He went on to describe his decision to purchase a large new household item for his wife. Once decided, he went about opening a new revenue stream to 'cover it.'

We're almost ready to move on from marketing and talk about new streams of income.

For now, complete this chapter on Money by brainstorming the worthy causes you would like to benefit as you add streams of revenue.

Name three or more foundations, charitable causes, or deserving people. Name the dollar amounts you'd like to give, then add today's date.

A Confused
Mind Always
Says No

As you absorb the thoughts and shifts around the Multiple Streams model of pursuing your coaching business, it may seem at first glance to be a fairly complex system.

And it's true, it's multi-faceted, and there is more than one way to start.

But I'm here to tell you that as you work your way through the information and exercises in this book, there are only two things I'd like you to focus on.

Get a Pink Spoon and put it on a One-Banana Website.

Get a Pink Spoon: As we discovered in the last chapter, a Pink Spoon, in your case, is a small sample of your expertise in the form of a free mini-information product. Done right, it gives your niche market a way to taste what you have to offer, and doesn't require you to trade time with each person interested in your offering.

One-Banana mini-sites are designed to present and elicit only one action from the visitor: signing up for your ecourse, ezine, or...you got it, Pink Spoon.

The beauty of the two steps you can immediately take is how very simple they are. Create a Pink Spoon, and put it on a simple one-page, 'one-banana' website.

In short, one-banana sites are crystal clear about their purpose. They are like a mailbox - when you walk up to one, you have absolutely ZERO doubt as to what to do. Why? Because there is only one thing to do. Open the slot and put your mail in.

There is a marketing principle out there that says 'a confused mind always says no.' Think of your product-based websites as online mailboxes. Create only one natural easy thing to do, and make it as obvious as possible.

When your initial sites follow the one-banana format, your visitors are much more likely to click through and ultimately become paying customers. There's only one thing to do (ie: sign up for your pink spoon), so that becomes, in fact, exactly what they do.

Many websites out there are what we call Portal sites. They are like an information booth, containing a number of pages and links - they work great as informational sites, but can cause overwhelm and are not as effective in terms of creating action.

There's a time and a place for Portal sites, but when you first start building a Multiple Streams Product Funnel, you'll get faster results and make the swiftest progress if you opt for the one-banana format.

Here are some examples of different styles of one-banana sites, all aimed at getting the visitor to take one, simple action. Each of them has been around long enough to have gathered stats to prove they work.

The Sign-up Site

This is an example of a freebie offering, or pink spoon. The purpose of this site is simple – to capture the visitor's email address.

**Jillian Middleton's Savvy Sponsoring.com
at www.SavvySponsoring.com.**

This site built an ezine list of of 400 subscribers in less than 3 months, without using pay-per-click advertising or other cash outlay.

How did Jillian do this? With a clear one-banana site and a very strong 'tell a friend' program - the original couple dozen people who were personally invited, invited their friends, who invited their friends, and so on...

Word of mouth is a powerful thing, but chances are if the site had not been as clear as it is, the subscriber list would not have grown as fast.

Can your next simple site follow this model?

Multiple Pink Spoons Pointing to One-banana

**Helen Lochore's Living in Winter Haven website:
LivingInWinterhaven.com**

In this site, you'll see that the entire page 'advertises' a whole bunch of pink spoons. But, look closely and you'll see that it is still a one-banana site - the only thing you can 'do' here is fill in your name and email address, BEFORE you can get all those pink spoons.

So, when a visitor fills in their name and email address, and clicks the 'Instant Access' button, this site immediately comes up:

http://livinginwinterhaven.com/welcome.htm

This site is optimized to build a relationship over time by using autoresponders. So, once someone fills in their email address to access the free resources, they are added to the autoresponder list and the relationship building begins.

About 10% of all visitors who reach the 'living in' page will give their email address to get the pink spoons. About 10% of those people end up buying with a realtor. This goes for nearly 200 websites that follow this model, all tested and tried. Every word on this site is there for a reason.

This is a first-rate model to test for anyone selling a higher priced service such as --- one-on-one coaching, anyone?

One-Banana Sales Pages

Even a long sales page with tons of content is considered a one-banana site, as long as there is only one thing to do on the given page. In the case of sales pages, all of the content leads to one action - buying the product.

San Mateo Coaching Event Page: www.ACoachingEvent.com

This is the sales letter we used for the San Mateo 3-Day Conference that took place in February 2005.

This site had a very short life, but during its time, it worked its little heart out. We launched this page January 7, and the event was February 4, 5 and 6. Within that time frame, there were about 2500 visits in total.

Of that number of visits, 125 people clicked the *Admit One* button and registered to come to the event. That's a 5% conversion.

If you are turned off by long sales pages, notice while you scroll this event page whether you feel engaged in conversation, and if you feel you leave with added value. Yes, long sales letters can be annoying, but this particular page was carefully crafted to be authentic, human and provide value – and the results proved its effectiveness.

So, long sales letters can be positive experiences both for the coach writing and for the visitor. When it comes to creating your own sales page using the one-banana philosophy, don't automatically write off making it a long one.

Consider how to write a sales page using a coaching approach – do what you can to ensure the reader leaves with more value (in the form of real content or new thoughts provoked) in ADDITION or ALONG THE WAY to clicking your one-banana.

Conversation Points

What does "A Confused Mind Always Says No" mean to you? What examples can you think of in your own life, where clarity supports action, and how can you translate this to your own web presence?

If your current website has more than one 'banana' on it, that's okay. It's more than fine to have a brochure site that has links to several bio pages, and so on. However when you're ready to sell a product, it will probably be time to add a new website to your collection. Is there one thing on your current website that you think might be good to give its own home? What is it and what would be the benefits of putting it on its own one-banana page?

Pause a moment and ask yourself "how much do you think it will cost to create a(nother) one-banana website?" If you named a figure over US$500, you very likely just saved yourself some money! A good direct response website that sells a product does not need to cost more than that. Write down the three next steps you need to do, to get yourself on the road to a profitable one-banana site.

Positioning

What does positioning mean?

Have a look at this diagram.

Figure 8: The Power Barbell

In the circle on the left, write the words "My Products/Services."

In the circle on the right, write the words "My Clients."

Now, draw a line that connects these two circles, straight across. Make it as straight as you can, and make sure it's a nice thick line.

What you have now, is what I call the 'Power Barbell.'

When you lift weights, or watch others do it, what is it that allows the lifter to lift more and more weight?

It's not the weight itself. It's the bar that holds the weight together, and in the case of the 'Power Barbell', it's the same thing.

Without a strong bar in the middle of the above two circles, you'll be missing a critical piece: a strong connection between your products and your clients.

Many people miss this piece.

This is, in short, the 'position' or stand you take towards your clients, that helps them understand why you are special, why you are different, and why they should care.
The position that Thomas Leonard used to take was that 'Everyone's a Coach.'

The position that the International Association of Coaches takes is to further the interests of coaching **clients** worldwide.

The position I take with Multiple Streams of Coaching Income is that 'There's a Coaching Solution to Every Problem' and that coaches should 'Stop Putting All Their Coaching 'Eggs' in One Basket.'

What is your position?

What do you stand for, in your market?

What is the boldest, most outrageous, most provocative position you can take in your niche?

We all know what it's like when local politicians seem to stand for nothing. It's boring, it's a non-event, and it's a sorry sight.

In your marketing, whatever niche you choose, I urge you take a position. The stronger your stand, the stronger your power barbell will be, and the more clients and products you'll be able to support.

An important additional note about positioning.

Great positioning is the key to writing great sales copy. As you create your own products, whether they are e-books or a coaching gym, you will soon try your hand at writing sales copy.

Try the following exercise for 10 minutes a day for the next three weeks, and you will be on your way to internalizing how to write good copy. All for the price of this book.

Find a great sales page. Make sure it's one that sells. It doesn't matter if you like it, but if you do, so much the better.

Take out a piece of paper and a pen, and transcribe the sales letter, word for word. Keep on writing until your ten minutes is up, or you get to a natural break in the letter.

Some things can't be taught, but they can be caught.

Writing great sales copy is one of those things. Sure you can learn some of it, but you'll pay a great deal of money for the privilege and with no guarantees.

Remember that a great sales letter is only great if it sells. And that no sales letter is ever carved in stone. The best internet marketers are constantly testing a new headline to see if they can convert more prospects into sales.

And some of the most unlikely sales letters bring in the most sales.

So practice feeding your brain great sales copy through your handwriting. It'll fire your neurons in a different way than they've ever fired before.

Like music, great sales letters have crescendos, a climax, and a natural fitting conclusion. These are the things you'll internalize as you do the transcribing.

The next time you put pen to paper to create sales letter for your product, you'll see a marked difference.

Be sure to let me know how it goes

Conversation Points

What are some strong positioning statements that you buy into? Make a list of the brands you support, whether they be clothing, kitchenware, houseware, vehicles, computers, other. What position does each of these brands take?

(Example: Nike's Just Do It.)

When you have made your biggest sales to date as a coach, what do you think has clinched the sale? How can you do more of that 'thing' that clinched it? Is that 'thing' your position statement? Should it be?

Zig-Zagging/ Being Remarkable

This chapter owes a lot to the teachings of Seth Godin, especially the ideas in his books *Purple Cow* and *Free Prize Inside*.'

If you haven't yet read Seth, it's brain food of the 'must' kind. Seth doesn't know it, but he's a coach. He sits around changing people's minds about things and getting them to take action. It's a remarkable living.

Zig-zagging isn't a term you'll find in the dictionary, unless maybe it's by Dr. Seuss.

It's actually a term my husband Mike made up to describe how we keep our relationship upbeat. I like to think it has a great application in online marketing.

Zig-zagging is about doing the unexpected. Fresh. To quote Mike, it goes something like, *"Just when you think I'm going to Zig, I Zag. It keeps the mystery in our marriage."*

It gets a laugh, and well, we have ten years of marital wonderment this year, so maybe its part of the magic.

Thus far, in terms of marketing, we've talked about how you can accelerate your ability to earn money by choosing a niche market. We've talked about identifying the problems that niche market wants to solve most. And we've also talked about taking a stand in your marketing materials.

Now, with zig-zagging, I'd like to take a moment to emphasize the importance of doing the unexpected.

What this means, in practical terms, is becoming intimate with your niche market and understanding how to get their attention. If everyone is doing X, you would be smart to do the opposite. If everyone is zagging, that's a great reason to do a little zig.

You see, it's important that you understand from the outset...there are no hard and fast rules in online marketing.

It's a bit disorienting to some, but it's true.

In fact, recently I overheard a new online entrepreneur say, *"I just wish I could have a list of 10 things to do each month, and then I could just do them."*

While I understood his sentiment, it doesn't really work that way.

The online marketer's world is a fluid, organic place.

Following a checklist of rules, or things to do, is a sure formula for becoming outdated and forgettable.

A perfect example is what author and coach Ramon Williamson

tested with one of his larger subscriber lists. He decided to send a broadcast with the subject line:

"Please unsubscribe."

You understand, this was diametrically opposite, and even shocking, because everyone else was concerning themselves with how many more subscribes they could find.

And Ramon's intent was completely serious. He was tired of people not taking action on his advice, and told them if that was going to be the case, they should unsubscribe. He only wanted to work with people who were ready to take action.

A great marketing move, right?

And a very coach-like move at that.

The thing is, this much-passed around broadcast of Ramon's definitely did not come from working on a checklist of things to do each month.

It came from understanding his market, knowing what would catch their attention, and having a bit of nerve to test something different.

A zig-zag move.

They're worth gold to you as a Multiple Streams Coach.

As you work to diversify, and stop putting all your eggs in one basket, you'll be glad you nurtured this approach.

As far as the person who just wished for a checklist, some days it can be easy to feel like that.

But let me tell it to you straight. If that's really what you're looking for, please, don't start working online, get a job instead.

On the other hand, if you're someone who enjoys staying on the balls of their feet...the better to move in any direction as the context warrants, you're going to have a wonderful time.

Some of the most enjoyable moments for me in my business are figuring out what the next 'fresh' approach is for me and my clients.

Whether it's posting a [NOT A PROMO] email to an email discussion list on Promo Day...

Not posting a fixed curriculum to the Multiple Streams membership is another zag move.

It's based on the idea that the best Multiple Streams material is just too fresh to post it too far in advance. Instead, I reserve the right to bring whatever is working best to members each month, at the moment it can really be said to be working...

As Seth likes to say, one of the greatest things about being an entrepreneur is that you are nimble. His advice:

"Test lots of things. Fail often."

The more you do that, the quicker and more frequently you'll find the 'play' that knocks it out of the proverbial park.

Integrate zig-zagging into your business thinking today.

Conversation Points

What are you doing currently that is forgettable to your audience? If your readers or prospects say 'So What?' you need to change things now.

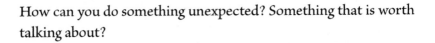

How can you do something unexpected? Something that is worth talking about?

You can try going to extremes in some way. Test the waters in a direction that's opposite to what most of your competitors are doing. Brainstorm with your Multiple Streams Conversation partners how your products can become remarkable.

Excuse Me, Can You Be My Google?

Moving on to a different topic that you should consider as you plan your marketing going forward.

Do you remember when radio disc jockeys used to be trusted friends?

Whenever they recommended a new recording artist, you would listen and often purchase that CD or cassette?

That disc jockey was a filter for you, someone you trusted to tell you what to pay attention to.

In a very real way, that's what we as coaches are. Coaches need to position themselves as filters for their clients. Why?

Human filters of this kind are becoming increasingly in demand.

- What should I read
- Who should I observe?
- What models work?

- How should I dress?
- Which artists are important?
- What charities are worthwhile?

The fact is people are no longer looking for more information. They are looking for the exactly right information at the precise moment they want it.

And they're looking for people they trust to find it.

As a coach, you have a real opportunity to become that trusted resource for your client through whatever product or service offering you offer.

Don't just give them information. Give them the right information, filtered, for them, and tell them you are doing so. This increases their perception of your value to them.

It's no coincidence that life is imitating, well, technology.

Online where there are billions of pieces of information, who has reigned supreme? Search engines like Google that make sense of the information and that filter the information.

Increasingly into the future, successful coaches will be human Googles for our clients. Human browsers.

As you go about picking your niche market, and delivering solutions to their problems, remember...your highest and best value to your client is in filtering the solutions that are perfect for them.

Think of yourself as a human browser. Begin positioning yourself as such.

Those of you who have read my personal observations about coaching, entrepreneurialism and Multiple Streams of Coaching Income will recognize this underlying principle in how I communicate most everything.

Not only does it make it easy for you to deliver your offerings, but it's exactly what your clients want from you.

Simple, right?

Oh and yes, whatever you do, be sure to stay away from delivering information for information sake.

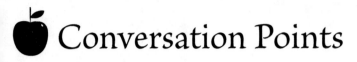

Conversation Points

What do you read? Why do you read it? Would your clients value knowing this? How can you share this filtered information with them?

Who are your Googles? What authors or other individuals do you trust to bring you information that you don't have to be on the hunt for? Why do you trust them?

Identify three new human Googles to add to your personal information filtering system. These can be magazine editors, bloggers, artists, authors, politicians, spiritual leaders or any other person or form of media.

Streams
of
Coaching
Income

Ebooks

Never underestimate the power of a well-written word.

Especially words written by a coach.

Tens of thousands of readers of coaching e-books have had their lives changed for the better by a well-written e-book.

It's a remarkable medium that you can tap into to coach others day or night, in the city or country, all across the planet.

Is writing an e-book for you?

Do you have the answers to a specific problem? Can you research the answers? Do you have a personal story to tell about overcoming the problem in your own life?

Is there a group of people for whom this problem is universal? A group of people who wake up in the night in a sweat, wishing, praying and wracking their brains for an answer?

The more they are in need of help, the more likely your e-book can change their lives.

Consider the e-book called *"A Eulogy to Remember, How To Write a Eulogy You'll Be Proud of in 5 Simple Steps"* of which author and coach Sheila Martin has sold several thousand copies in the last few years.

The group of people Sheila has helped has made itself known through the hundreds of stories she has collected about how much her 77 pages have helped.

People who have had a death in the family.

Just a very little market research shows that more than 100,000 people searched for information of some sort about funerals and death in the family, in the last 30 days alone.

This is the niche, or group of people that Sheila's e-book serves, to the exclusion of all others.

She doesn't serve brides, acupuncturists, bulldog owners, young divorcees, or bareback horseback riders.

Sheila's book answers a very specific problem, the anxious task of writing a eulogy for those who have recently had a death in the family.

Over 15,000 searches were done specifically for how to write a eulogy in that same time period.

So you can see that the formula Niche + Problem + Format = Income Stream is played out very clearly in this example.

And as a result, more than two thousand families have been coached through the trying but precious task of honoring their loved ones.

All in the 77 pages of an e-book that sits on a website around the clock, available, not by appointment, nor by filling in an application. Just available at the precise moment a person needs it, period.

"Sheila, I can't tell you what a great help your e-book was in helping me write a tribute to my Mom. (She) was an incredible lady and I was just praying that I could do justice to her memory.

(Eulogies with Love) not only helped me with the writing, but also with the delivery. I was able to control my emotions (which is very hard for me to do), and followed all of your suggestions for staying calm during her funeral service.

I can't thank you enough for writing this wonderful book that has helped so many families.

In actual fact, Sheila has become a multiple streams maven, authoring additional niche titles such as "*Happy Hysterectomy*" – also an ebook – and a new title coming out on the topic of healing from fibromyalgia.

Sheila's own words sum it up like no others can:

"My first eBook required a LOT of learning and effort up-front, but now each one is easier. And they are all like little oil wells – continuing to send me money day after day."

That's to the tune of more than $10,000 per month in gross income, to be exact, and now that Sheila is able to outsource customer service and traffic generation, she anticipates being able to double and triple that figure in a very short time.

What is Sheila's very best advice to the aspiring Multiple Streams coach?

"Invest wholeheartedly in the initial learning from the very best online teachers...and then take massive action."

I couldn't have said it better myself, thank you Sheila.
To find out more about Sheila's Eulogy eBook, go to EulogyHelp-Desk.com. And stay tuned. Sheila is converting this offering into a multimedia offering, another example of a profound stream of coaching you too can create. But more on that in a later chapter. If you think writing an e-book is for you, this is what you need to know:

1. A great e-book is not long.

In fact, the very best e-books are 10-35 pages long, and no longer.

Why is this?

In keeping with the Multiple Streams Formula of Niche + Problem + Packaging, the e-book that is short and sweet answers in a laser-like fashion the problem that the reader wants to solve.

It's the most valuable e-book a client can buy because you have filtered the exact information they most need, and cut out the rest.

Don't make the mistake of thinking you need 100 pages to call yourself an e-book publisher. Cut to the chase.

Pretend you have a one-on-one client and you only have 15 minutes to shift that person. It's the same with an e-book.

Besides, sales statistics bear it out. The longer e-books just aren't cutting the mustard when it comes to sales anymore. And it's not really a surprise. People want fast results, so when you go to design your e-book, make sure you remember that.

Besides, it just means you're that much closer to being finished right?

2. A marketable e-book is very specific.

This goes hand in hand with #1.

Don't write e-books that are general. They just aren't marketable and you'll be in for a heartache.

The key to marketability is communicating to specific people that your answer is the precise one they need.

So taking the lead from Eulogy Writing Coach Sheila, above, an e-book about 'How to Write' would not be marketable. An e-book that is very specific, 'How to Write a Eulogy' on the other hand, has terrific marketability because it answers a specific problem.

Note: Big time folk with lots of money in their marketing budget can write general things and sell them; because they already have a customer following that will buy.

Iconic figures such as the Pope, Former President Jimmy Carter, or say pop-culture leaders such as Oprah Winfrey could write a book on just about anything, and sell.

But for most coaches who are building their businesses from scratch, specificity is shortcut to reaching your audience, and, by association, the way to sales.

(Even prolific and well-known author Dan Poynter's best-selling title is "*Self-Publish Your Book*"...specific in its own way.)

3. A great coaching e-book uses a coaching approach.

Take some time as you prepare to write your e-book, and do two things:

Read great e-books.

The e-books used as examples in this book are coaching e-books selected to illustrate what works. As you read, take notes on what techniques work, what don't.
Then take what you know works as a coach, and transfer that to your e-book.

As a coach, do you harness the power of the provocative question in your one-on-one coaching calls?

Perhaps you have a special ability to see the greater truth in a client's life?

/ Take special note of what makes your coaching exceptional in one mode of delivery and deliberately set out to translate that to the writing you do for your e-book.

I'm still looking for a 25-page e-book that exemplifies in its pages the 15 Coaching Proficiencies by CoachVille, for example. It doesn't matter what topic you choose, make it a coaching e-book.

Tens of thousands of e-books are downloaded each year.

Of those, short, specific e-books that take a coaching approach are changing lives for the better every day. Will you accept the challenge to make yours one of them?

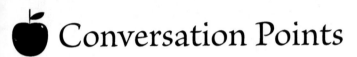 # Conversation Points

What e-books have you read recently? Which ones did you most enjoy and why? Do any of them take a coaching approach?

How can you incorporate a coaching approach into your writing? In what ways can you make your articles, e-books, and any other writing representative of a one-on-one coaching session with you?

Ecourses

Have you ever heard of the book *Everything Men Really Know About Women* by Ken Debono?

It was published in 1996 and clocks in at 200 pages.

If you have the chance to look at a copy somewhere, have a flip through.

You'll notice that inside the bright blue cover, all but four pages are completely blank.

Wry smiles aside, there is a greater lesson in the blank pages of this book than you might think, and it has to do with the power of silence and blank space.

As we all know, there is just so much information in the world these days, and successful coaches around the world have become skilled at making sure there is ample learning and integrating space.

Furthermore, inherent in the one-on-one coaching relationship is the fact that there is usually a week or more time that goes by between each coaching call. That's the space in which everything happens.

In the bigger picture, we talk a great deal about meditation, and exploring the gap between our thoughts. Spiritual leaders everywhere are proponents of a daily habit of silence.

What's interesting is that eCourses, by their very nature, are a time-release format of delivering material that lends itself perfectly to the idea that silence is important.

eCourses are small pieces of writing delivered to readers one piece at a time via email. Using auto responder technology, the lessons can be delivered with a specific interval of time in between.

Oftentimes, an e-Book which is just one long piece of material, can be nicely chunked down into smaller pieces, and delivered in eCourse style to great effect. (Or indeed vice versa.)

You see, creating Multiple Streams of Coaching Income doesn't have to mean more work, or time spent creating products. In fact, leveraging one piece of writing into multiple formats is simple, and because everyone likes things in different formats, this works out perfectly.

Chartered Financial Consultant and Financial Freedom Coach Kelly Reese is a great example of this. He delivers an eCourse program called 'Retire Quickly' by email for $50, and also offers audio, live seminar, and membership versions of these same nuggets of wisdom.

Just one of his literally tens of thousands of readers from over 100 different countries says:

"Kelly, I have been in traditional business all my life. I am President of our family business, located in a very rural and beautiful community in Indiana.

The practical financial education and tools you have provided in the "How to Retire Quickly" eCourse have provided me with a new perspective as to how I manage both my business and personal finances.

You are right, Kelly, "One really can retire in 7 years or less." Simply follow the Retire Quickly eCourse one-step at a time.

Thanks, Kelly,
Joe Huber, Jr."

The profound effect of this material, in a coaching format that has time to soak into a person's life, is key to the success of programs such as these.

Especially well suited to changing lives, the eCourse is the unsung hero of coaching formats, period, and as such, presents an opportunity for you.

✓ Put simply:

An eCourse is simple to write.

Each lesson is a simple article. Write between 5-10 lessons and you have a terrific eCourse on your hands.

If you find it easier to write a Top 10 list, as many coaches do, try that, and then chunk each bullet point into one lesson. And there you have it.

An eCourse is a perfect relationship-builder and lead generator.

As they say in sales circles, it often takes seven times before a customer says 'yes' and opens his wallet. A multi-issue eCourse is built to give repeat occasions for the customer to check out the coach, and purchase other products, whereas other one-off items may not.

As they say in relationship circles, it may take you more than one date to get a kiss. Once again, an eCourse is a coaching format that allows your customer to get to know you before hiring you for something else.

Although eCourses for pay are being used effectively to generate revenue in dozens of coaching businesses, they are the quintessential lead generator when used as a freebie.

An eCourse is a powerful mirror of the coaching process.

It allows a space in between lessons so that action can be taken, and new ideas integrated.

Written by a talented coach, a good eCourse can bridge the gap between the reader knowing something, and that same reader applying it to their lives. Just like the weekly coaching session.

How does one accomplish this? Quite simply, by capitalizing on the time that elapses between lessons... the silences.

In other words, if your eCourse is 10 lessons, be sure to close each lesson off powerfully. At the end of the lessons, design an exercise, a call to action, an invitation or assignment that lets the reader live with the concepts you've just shared before the next one arrives.

Let me put it to you another way. Have you ever listened to a piece of music, perhaps something classical, and noticed the silence between the notes? Maybe it's the silence after a particularly stirring bit of energetic violin, and there is a very full moment of silence that anticipates the next note?

That's what the silence that occurs between lessons in an eCourse is like. And that's where tremendous shifts can be made.

✓ Great coaches know how to build up the gap between the lessons.

Like internet marketer Ken McCarthy who writes more than a dozen eCourses that reach anywhere up to thousands of people around the world every day.

One of his eCourses, which he delivers by auto responder, is particularly powerful at 'milking' the silence between lessons. Ken writes it in a way that activates my mind even when I'm not reading his words. Check it out at **www.KenMcCarthy.com**

That's the power a great coach taps into.

If you look at each lesson as a simple article, how long would it take you to complete 10?

Write your eCourse.

Conversation Points

When was the last time you had a personal breakthrough that led you to greater levels of success? What were the circumstances that enabled that breakthrough to happen? Was silence, meditation or prayer a part of it?

How do you use the time between one-on-one coaching sessions to create breakthroughs for your clients?

In what way could the creation of an eCourse serve your Multiple Streams business?

Here are a few additional sample eCourses:

- Michelle Biton, PregnancywithoutPounds.com *"Pregnancy Without Pounds"* eCourse

- Tina Forsyth, GrowYourVABiz.com *"The 10 Critical Skills for a Thriving Virtual Assistant Practice"* eCourse

- Joe Taylor Jr., MusicBizCoaching.com *"Five day crash course for success as a WORKING musician"*

- Bob Cobb, UltimateFinancialAdvisor.com *"The Competitive Edge"* 5-part ecourse.

- Andrea Lee, SixtoSevenFigures.com *"5 Keys to Reaching Seven Figures in Business - For Companies That Inspire For a Living"*

Which of these did you enjoy most and why? What elements will you emulate, and what elements will you edit out?

Print Books

Print books are the crème de la crème of intellectual achievement, aren't they?

They are like the Mt. Everest of accomplishments.

And hundreds of books are being written in the personal development field each year, some using a coaching approach more than others.

Remember the litmus test of a coaching approach is that the book ✓ causes real and lasting action in a person's life.

The beauty of a print book is that you can go deep into all areas, and use all sorts of coaching techniques throughout. A book is to coaching as a boot camp is to live training. Intense, focused, and in depth, the reader really commits when they pick up your book, and you have the chance to make some really deep shifts.

That said, I could wish for more great coaching books in print, each focused on solving a problem for a niche market, and of course, the more general variety of inspirational book as well...tied into action, of course.

There are some terrific ones already, such as Suzanne Falter Barnes' *How Much Joy Can You Stand?* which has sold more than 60,000 copies worldwide.

Its particular coaching approach is reflected in each of its readers:

"One of the things I like best about it is that you can get so much out of just reading one chapter, or engaging in one exercise. You don't need to read the whole thing at once to benefit."

"The book has helped me tremendously in many ways, including getting me refocused on a major book project I had been lost and confused about for some time. In this slim book, Suzanne Falter-Barns packs the support of a great coach and an entire cheerleading squad. It is a joy to read this book and re-connect with your creative spirit as a result of that. I will return to it when I hit even the tiniest inner road blocks."

Author Suzanne is justifiably delighted at the reach of her book, saying her hopes are that ripple effects of the book will be huge. She writes each of her books with the intention of helping others dig into their dreams.

Find out more about it at **www.HowMuchJoy.com**

A book is indeed a powerful way to change lives and doesn't have to be hard.

Just a few tips to illuminate the way:

If you are a coach doing one-on-one sessions, try writing an article after each weekly session. What was the problem? What were the solutions offered? What were the action items or key shifts?

Do this for each coaching session you hold, for several months. After that time, have a look at your collection of articles, and step back. Rough out a structure, title and topic that adequately 'holds' the articles you've written. Then make a list of articles you need to add, to properly set the context for your articles, and a conclusion.

Throughout your book, weave in opportunities for your reader to interact with you. Although the pages of a book are stagnant, your reader's mind is not. The more ways you give your reader to engage in action as a result of your book, the more your book acts as your surrogate 'coach' even though you aren't physically there, on the telephone or otherwise.

So not only at the end of each chapter, but throughout the pages in your book, ask questions, invite journaling, brainstorming or list making. Encourage conversations with a fellow reader, even suggest a meditation exercise. As a coach you have a unique talent for waking people up. Make a conscious effort to use this talent in the pages of your book, and what you'll have is not just a best-seller, but a true blue coaching book, a beautiful thing.

There you have two methods of capturing the essence of great coaching in a book. For most coaches in one-on-one practice, the first technique is often overlooked. Build this practice into your daily routine and what will naturally result is a great book product.

That's it!

While you're at it, have a look at this book. It was built on the same philosophy outlined above.

And hey, why not take a moment and make a few notes on what elements you see here that you like, so you can integrate them into your best seller!

With the advent of print on demand services, self-publishing opportunities and especially the ability to market online cheaply and quickly, I'm looking for a multitude more coaching books in short order, and I hope at least one of them is yours.

You may just find an opportunity to showcase yours in an online coaching catalog I'm creating.

It's slated to receive a steady stream of thousands of visitors who are primed to improve their lives through coaching-related products and I'll be taking submissions first from Multiple Streamers.

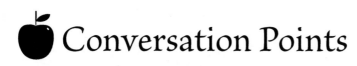 Conversation Points

Writing a book opens doors to speaking engagements, media opportunities, and general buzz around your brand and niche market. Brainstorm ideas for a book that's inside you. Remember 100 pages is plenty.

Ironically, most books written for coaches are not coach-like. They're dense texts that don't foster conversation. If you were to write a coach-like book, what elements would you include that would make it as similar to a coaching session with you as possible?

Here are just a few additional great books written with a coaching approach:

- *Break Free From Burnout*, Mary P. Lewis
- *Be Heard Now*, Lee Glickstein

Online Memberships

Have you ever noticed geese flying overhead, whether that be south for the winter, or back home in the spring?

In Canada where I live, this is a regular sight and a sure sign of the seasons passing.

From time to time, it's easy to notice that there is a certain pattern to the flying geese. Often, they fly in formation, in a shape that makes it easier to fly as a group than alone, something that conserves energy for the trip.

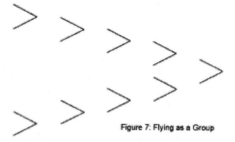

Figure 7: Flying as a Group

Online memberships, when built right, are built on the same philosophy, even though they consist of bits, bytes, pixels and websites and not beaks, feathers or wings.

Have you noticed that things are easier to do when you're surrounded by like-minded people going for the same goal?
Training for a marathon seems less onerous when you run with a bunch of buddies.

A garage sale seems like too much bother until the neighborhood holds one together.

And of course, goals become so much more achievable when there's a coach in the picture.

An online membership usually consists of a private website available to a certain set of people with common interests and goals.

Much like a library, online memberships take on a certain form, often containing resources such as books, magazines, articles, and even audio and video materials.

Premium membership sites will often integrate a personal touch by providing support from a real person, whether that is by email, help desk or at a discussion board.

At its most elaborate, membership websites can leak over into the offline world, and members who were previously cyber-buddies only meet face-to-face for the first time and the bonds get cemented. These tend to be memberships that have the most longevity online...they achieve this by weaving in real meetings so the online connection takes on a new dimension.

Coaching is being done in online memberships now in many different markets.

Teamwork coach Tom Heck has been operating his for some two years now, and has 600 members in over 64+ countries, all focused on making teamwork a part of their lives and work.

In his first years of operation, his pricing structure has ranged from $19.95 for a lifetime, to $79 per year. Considering the tremendous value of his offering, Tom reports he will soon be moving Teach-MeTeamwork.com to a monthly fee structure at $19.95/month.

The Multiple Streams of Coaching Income membership is now more than 150-member strong and putting real money in coaches' pockets with every passing month.

The Newbie Club membership for technology training online now supports more than 100,000 members.

The fact is online memberships of all sizes and shapes are a very effective way of building a supportive environment. Environments that support us make things easier to achieve.

Although you may think that the supportive environment supports the members, but in fact one of the hidden benefits of a membership is it channels the energy of the coach in 'charge.'

Whereas a coach who is creating an e-book this month can get away with being late, the demands of a membership often lead to steadier production of new materials. So as host of the membership you get pulled forward too.

When a goose flies out of formation, it suddenly feels the drag and resistance of trying to go it alone.

When it returns to formation, it can take advantage of the pull of the group to get where it wants to go with less effort.

When designing an online membership, a key factor is tapping into one of the strongest forces in the human personality...the desire to belong.

In Tom's Teach Me Teamwork membership program, he's created a common meeting place, a website, where members from over 64 countries meet, and through the coaching environment he's built at his site, achieved tremendous things:

> *"As a camp director, I supervise 100 staff and am responsible for overseeing programs that serve over 2700 youth every summer.*
>
> *Teaching and leading activities that build community and enhance team skills is an integral part of my job. The [Teach-MeTeamWork Online Membership] site has provided me with tons of great ideas that I can put to use immediately in the camp setting for training of staff and for team building with our youth."*
>
> Van Van Horne,
> Program Director for Lutheridge+Lutherock Camp

Particularly if you are a coach who enjoys building intimate relationships with your customers, but doesn't want to limit yourself to the one-on-one coaching session, the online membership site can create a very long-lasting relationship with many people worldwide, using the leverage of the Internet.

When considering new streams of coaching income, online memberships have certain significant characteristics:

A membership site gives your clients access to the information they need, when they want it, not just when you are available by telephone.

A membership site gives your clients access to each other, and the body of knowledge they represent, which can be enormous. The powerful connections that are made are very good fodder for a multidimensional coaching experience for your clients.

A membership site can be demanding to maintain, since new content and material need to be developed to ensure the membership is fresh and up to date.

Because a membership site doesn't have a beginning, middle, and end, it is an excellent long-term relationship builder, which allows you to serve your clients in multiple ways with multiple products.

E-books, ecourses, teleseminars...over the time period that your members remain with you, it's highly likely they will purchase more than one thing for you, which keeps your profit margins high.

You can bill a recurring fee for access to your online membership site. Some sites are lifetime membership sites, but most memberships follow the subscription model.

For example, if you subscribe to Fast Company magazine, you know that you pay a certain dollar amount each month in exchange for a fresh set of 100+ pages.

The same goes for membership sites. Yearly or monthly membership fees allow you to project cash flow with much greater accuracy than one-off sales of e-books, for example.

Best of all, the magic of a great online membership really occurs when a sense of community can flourish:

> *"I was initially struck by Tom's energy and passion for working with children, for working with teams and for building a community where all could meet and share best practices. [...] Tom [...] has created an environment where people trust and believe in generosity. Tom presented to my virtual community of team coaches and they too are enthusiastically benefiting from the wonderful Teach Me Teamwork Community that Tom has built. Thank you, Tom, for being our champion."*

> Cynder Niemela, MA, MBA, Master Certified Coach,
> High Impact Teaming, LLC

> *"Joining Multiple Streams has been pointless...unless you count my increased e-Book sales, creation of new products & services almost daily, synergy with other members, and being supported in positive, realistic ways... I find myself playing a MUCH Bigger Game..."*
> David Flack | TheAcceleratorCoach.com

'Cyber-belongingness' is no longer just a trend.

With more than a million people in the world now identifying themselves with one of thousands of online groups, online memberships are modern 'tribes' that are filling the gaps being left by neighborhoods and even church groups of old.

Building memberships with heart, soul, intellect, and embracing a coaching approach throughout, is a powerful way of leading as a coach.

Not to mention one of the best ways an internet savvy Multiple Streams coach can build a business with positive cash flow.

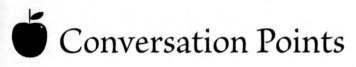 # Conversation Points

What online memberships have you been part of? What were the elements you most prized? Why?

Is an online membership offering for you? If yes, what are your first three practical action steps?

If you hesitate to build a membership site as part of your Product Funnel, list your reasons here and discuss them with a conversation partner the next time you have an opportunity.

Live Trainings, Workshops & Retreats

When preparing to speak at an internet marketing conference in Florida this year, I learned that the average adult cannot stay still for more than seven minutes.

Isn't it ironic that that's the amount of time you'll probably take to read this chapter?

The next time you are at a live training or workshop, take a moment to notice.

If the training is occurring lecture-style, you'll easily spot the shifting and fidgeting that is as textbook for adults as squirming and jiggling is for kids.

If the training is experiential in nature, and uses questions, group work, written exercises, and lots of interactive elements, you're much more likely to see the smooth energized movements of adults in the happy learning zone.

In-person trainings are quite simply a magnificent opportunity for coaches. Magnificent because of three main things:

1. The face-to-face element allows learners to get a three-dimensional experience of you, your energy and your style...this can be just the thing to solidify coaching relationships that will take place by phone or virtually the rest of the time...

2. The group setting allows all types of learners to truly engage with your material, and leverage the collective knowledge and energy of the group, rather than focusing solely on the coach.

3. The in-person format lends itself well to following-up with participants 'after the show'...this gives coaches a real opportunity to help participants make shifts from simply knowing something to taking real action on it AND generate significant streams of income over and above the workshop itself.

In fact, if you're seriously considering live trainings as one of your long-term streams of coaching income, know this:

Live events are one of the most lucrative streams of income there are. Not only because of the training fees but because for whatever reason, live venues are proven places to sell a great deal of additional product and service.

Added to that, live training has also proven to be quite a recession proof activity.

Exciting opportunity for a coach, right?

It's true. And knowing that, it's still pretty unbelievable how many day long workshops are presented without a drop of real connection.

Although the participants are physically there, often what transpires is sadly not much more valuable than listening to a CD recording.

With no planned time to shake hands with the person sitting in front or behind, the event once over, is over.

That said, this is good news for coaches. When workshops or seminars are held using a coaching approach, they are remarkably more memorable and effective.

As a result, they get talked about like crazy, and the coach leading the event reaps the rewards of a ton of viral word of mouth marketing without spending a cent.

Just ask HollywoodCoach.com's David Brownstein about the kind of feedback he gets:

"David, thank you very much for speaking to our Women In Film Santa Barbara Networking Breakfast.

It was the first meeting of its kind for us. That is, interactive. It was very exciting to see everyone responding, asking questions, giving advice and helping the others around them.

Normally when a meeting is finished everyone jumps up and rushes the speaker to get as much "me" information as possible. This was the exact opposite. Though people did speak one-on-one with you later on, it was amazing that at the end of this meeting no one rushed you. They were more concerned with speaking with their "partner" and "newest best friend." People were helping each other instead of focusing on their own needs and interests.

I feel that it was the most life-changing, decision-making meeting we have ever had.

The morning was a tremendous success, David. Teaching us how to live the balanced life, how to prioritize, how to say no, and how to help the person next to us is the best kind of meeting!! All that in one hour! Your seminars must be completely fantastic!

Thank you, too, for your informative handouts and your inspirational Circle of Life.

Sincerely,

Laurel Walsh, Chair | Leslie Gangl Howe, Co-Chairs

Now those are some musical words!

By bringing this kind of experiential impact to his in-person coaching workshops and trainings, David is transforming the lives of Hollywood Executives one person at a time.

And because Pop Culture Executives play such a profound role in communicating ideas and values in our society, this is coaching with real reach.

Of course the side benefit of a coaching event like David's is that because everyone's already moving around, raising their hands and passing around a microphone, no one needs to fidget -- a beautiful thing!

As you design your next coaching-based live training, there is just one simple thing you can do to make sure you knock it out of the park, and maximize your earnings:

Add a 'post-training' element

For example:

David Brownstein will be a STAR SPEAKER at Screenwriters Expo 3 on Nov 5 - 7, 2004, and the DAY AFTER on Nov 8th for a special presentation designed to help you stay in action after the expo.

After the Expo . . . The Action Plan!
You've got the talent, the passion, and now the information. Don't let your momentum fade out! In this highly interactive, informative and inspiring planning session you will: Synthesize all you've learned at Expo 3, meet other writers from your area and develop a structure of accountability and support, and design your own individual action plan to guarantee your success.

Monday, November 8
10 AM to 4 PM @ The Convention Center
$75.00 (includes follow up telephone support phone call)

This can take on many formats such as a 5, 10 or 12-week follow up coaching program as a bonus to participants. You can make all or part of it for an additional fee.

Or, it can be project-based such as the 'Complete Your Info-Product within 12-Days after the Conference' Challenge that Coach Ramon Williamson held after Willie Crawford's Internet Marketing How to Weekend.

Or maybe you design a quarterly training cycle so you meet face to face once every 90 days, and participants become members of a training club.

Whatever format you create, the key point here is that by leveraging the energy of a live event, you can open new revenue streams that market themselves at the event, AND impact a whole lot of happy people.

Even if your live training is only one-hour on a week day evening, the connection the participants have with you is stronger at that moment than it will be again. Don't miss the chance to get a commitment to work with you after the evening is over.

In fact, make it a point to never go out in public without a few offerings at various price points, and an easy way to order via a one-page sign up sheet.

Whether that is a CD, a booklet, or a more expensive item, doesn't matter.

It's human nature to want a souvenir of a good experience. You, as a coach, need to be ready to provide that souvenir.

Other than that, simply do your homework, and prepare yourself to go against some of the more conventional training practices. Instead...

- Use PowerPoint but only if it contains visual images for emphasis.

- Tell stories, personal ones that relate to the topic, and bring the message home on an emotional level.

- Be brave, and be very real. Don't perform. Let the real you out.

- Go to smaller centers to speak, or speak locally. Traveling to the big six cities is not the only way to go.

- Consider pricing carefully according to your purpose. If the training will be a platform from which to gain more business, you may want to price the training itself quite low, and consider it a 'loss leader.'

- Hire a wedding or student videographer to capture your event on film. This will form the basis of another product for your product funnel.

- Prepare an agenda, but leave lots of breathing room. Stay flexible; let the audience tell you when it wants to detour off the agenda.

- Go the extra mile to connect participants with each other, not just with you. The relationships that result will reflect back on your ability to provide room and space to make that happen.

- Last but not least, make it interactive, and include lots of laughter.

There is an intimacy that comes with being in the same room together for a length of time with the goal of opening our hearts and minds. Much like sharing a meal with friends, face-to-face events are special occasions.

And laughter is the best reward you can give the person who's given you the gift of their physical presence.

Coach on.

Conversation Points

Many coaches like the idea of going on a speaker tour. If this is you, try designing a Product Funnel around speaking. Reverse engineer the other levels in your funnel to support the speaking part.

Multiple Streams coaches will find getting booked to speak to groups much easier than others.

The reason for this is that you are willing to speak for no fee. Instead, your offer to the host organization is that you will speak for no fee provided you can collect the email addresses of attendees, and offer them products from your Product Funnel for purchase.

Make a list of at least five organizations to contact with this offer, and set a goal of a certain number of speaking engagements in the next 90 days. Which groups will you try first?

TeleSeminars

Hey, as you read this, what can you hear?

Is it the sound of silence? Hmm, probably not.

Well, let me ask you this then. What, in your opinion, does coaching **s o u n d** like?

That's right. If coaching was a sound, what would that sound be?

It's an interesting question for a chapter on TeleSeminars for several reasons. The growing trends for the next foreseeable years are about the five senses: sight, sound, smell, touch and taste.

In the computer/telephony world where much of coaching takes place, it can be a bit of a mind boggle to consider how the five senses play in.

But when it comes to TeleSeminars, I have to pause.

There is actually something rather mysterious about a TeleSeminar, isn't there?

A certain intimacy that's created in the sound of voices gathering together, that creates a depth of connection unlike one that you make when face-to-face.

Maybe because it's a bit of an out of body experience, being on a TeleSeminar, that makes the connection seem almost spiritual at times.

And that's the quality I think best characterizes the sound of coaching. It's the sound of deep conversations and advanced communicating.

Why do I say all this?

TeleSeminar programs are the number one most versatile method of building business available to coaches period.

And the WAY in which you hold them - in other words, the style and sound that characterizes your TeleSeminars, is going to be (or continue to be) a big part of your brand.

If music is the soundtrack to our life, I suggest that TeleSeminars for your clients will become the conscience.

Uppermost in my mind when it comes to the sound of coaching is the importance of silence, a powerful tool in any top-notch TeleSeminar.

When you next listen to music, try listening not to the notes or melody, or a particular voice or instrument.

Instead listen to the pauses and rests...the moments of silence between the notes.

Without those silences, if all we heard was one continuous note with no pauses, this wouldn't be music, but noise.

And the same goes with verbal communication, especially on TeleSeminars.

Whether you are one-on-one with a single client on the telephone, or you're on a large conference line with more than 100 listeners for company, I encourage you to leave room for more silence, so that the 'ahas' have space to breathe.

Of all the things that Thomas Leonard did, did you realize that most all of it had a foundation of TeleSeminars?

I didn't click either, not until well into my time as General Manager of CoachVille.

If you're someone who took the very early TeleSeminars with Thomas, you can vouch for this, I know.

It was with the start of a TeleSeminar series, for example, on the Principles of Attraction, which generated the content for the Portable Coach.

It was a series of TeleSeminars that gave a start to Coach U, the first coach training organization of its kind.

And it was TeleSeminars that birthed CoachVille and the Schools of Coaching as well...through Future of Coaching calls, TeleClass Leader Trainings and well, all of it.

Without the TeleSeminar, it's not an exaggeration to say that in fact, the coaching profession, with all its training organizations, etc., might simply not be.

I guess it's obvious too that by extension, since most coaching takes place by phone, we owe a lot to Alexander Graham Bell.

And so in pondering these facts...I have a suggestion for you.

As you are reading your way through this book, jotting whatever notes down, brainstorming your next steps as a Multiple Streams Coach, let me suggest that your strategy definitely include TeleSeminars in one or more of places.

In fact, in every marketing funnel, at every level, and for whatever topic, there is a function for a TeleSeminar that will lead to more sales, stronger streams of income and of course, greater reach.
It's true, I'm hard pressed to think of a coaching business with any vision that does not include TeleSeminars.

Moreover, TeleSeminars can be a great low-risk way to test a new product idea. This quarter, I tested an Ezine Makeover TeleSeminar to good effect...its goal was Making Over Your Coaching Ezine So It Makes You Money.

Based on the results of the class, this will become a passive product with a one-session coaching add-on for those who wish it. People – coaches too – love to see before and after results.

In other words, I'm not saying TeleSeminars are a panacea, a cure for all ills, but if you ever run into a marketing problem, or a stuck point in your marketing funnel...it's likely that a strategically applied Teleseminar offering will unplug you in a jiffy.

Cases in point, based on real successes mostly with consulting clients to date:

- When 2-day live events are not filling as well you like, set up a free TeleSeminar title to introduce the content of the event, and secure early registrations from participants by offering a 'listener only' timed discount of $20.

- If you find new members in your online community getting frustrated and requesting refunds, implement a complimentary 'Welcome' TeleSeminar that acts as a Welcome Wagon, allays initial confusion and boosts retention.

- Perhaps your e-Book sales are slow this month. Pick three points from the e-Book itself and design a conversational TeleSeminar around this, with the goal to boost sales.

- Stuck on what your next information product offering should be? Hold an 'Open House' TeleSeminar where your listeners are invited to ask you anything they want. Take careful notes of their questions and tailor your next product around the things they most want.

- Want to say a special thank you to your customers? A bonus TeleSeminar with an invited guest can do the trick nicely, and all with little effort from you.

Hey, here's a thing. If you are stuck marketing something and you think you can stump me with, "I bet you can't fix this with a TeleSeminar strategy!" send along the challenge and if you're right, I'll send you a free copy of the book that you can share with a friend.

Now here are a few golden rules for running TeleSeminars:

For student interaction or any coaching demos or hot seats, a 40-person maximum per call is a good rule of thumb.

As internet marketers increasingly cotton onto the power of Tele-Seminars, you'll see more and more people climbing onto a bridge at once...150 people and more.

This is a great strategy especially when there is a high-profile guest being interviewed, for example, but more often than not, the reason so many people are allowed onto one call is because they can.

For internet marketers with truly big-shot pulling power, it makes bottom-line sense to put as many people on the calls as possible.

From a coaching perspective, only do calls larger than 40 people when you are happy to have little to no interaction.

Use some techniques to increase attendance in your no-fee Tele-Seminars.

Holding complimentary TeleSeminars is a tried-and-tested method of educating students on the benefits of one of your other products or services.

But where many initial efforts at this fall short is in getting registered students to actually show up on the call. Because it's a free class, many people will register, only to skip the class later because it's no skin off their back.

In fact, unless you are proactive about it, you can generally expect between 25-50% of registrants to 'no-show' for a freebie class.

So what can you do to encourage attendance in spite of that? There are many creative things to experiment with - here are just two:

1. Set up pre-class reminder emails one day in advance, and the day of the class. In the reminder emails include an offer of some kind that will be available only to those who attend the class.

This could take the form of a question, 'Would you like a recommendation to the most reliable shopping cart system available?' 'I look forward to sharing the link with you at class time. Here's the number to dial.'

Or it could take the form of an offer 'Be sure to call in for your class. I have a time sensitive offer I'll be making that will save you $20.'

2. Enroll the students in the process of building the class. When you announce the class, offer them a special report or audio excerpt that reinforces the benefits of the class. When the sign-up, send them the report or audio along with a question:

'What are the three most important questions you have about changing careers and starting your own business?'

'We'll compile your questions and answer as many of them as possible on the TeleSeminar.'

To get their own questions answered on the call, more people will actually dial the number of the call when the time comes.

Remember, one of the key benefits of TeleSeminars is the highly leveraged use of your time.

In fact, if you haven't done so already, I suggest you stop doing free introductory coaching calls, and switch to a TeleSeminar format instead. By speaking with more than one person at a time, you instantly increase the value of your time.

It goes without saying that the more people who register and actually turn up for your TeleSeminar, the better for you.

Pay close attention to how well your free TeleSeminars are converting into sales for you.

As a Multiple Streams coach there is no reason why each TeleSeminar should not gross you several hundred or more dollars each time.

Accomplish this by making a time-sensitive offer at the end of the TeleSeminar. Provide an exclusive discount of some sort for attendees of the call if they register within 24 hours. Sweeten the pot further by adding bonuses to the offering.

And by delivering terrific TeleSeminar content in the first place, you demonstrate the value you'll provide in your pay offering.

It works; it's been done for years by many very highly successful coaches of all stripes in all markets. Ace coaches even reach conversion rates as high as 60-80% into a pay offering.

Try it; I think you'll like it. And along the way, you'll discover new ways to convert your students into buyers. When you find one that works, keep doing it. Those new ways are gold and will become the lifeblood of your business.

Last but not least, cultivate a style of TeleSeminar leading.

Start by attending classes yourself. Then cultivate a style that conveys your authority on the subject in a way that showcases your personal style.

Some coaches swear by over delivering to the max, and filling the classes with content to the brim.

Other coaches are adamant that there be 25% content, and the rest of the time be given to discussion.

You'll find your way. Listen hard to your audience, and you'll more than find your way.

There are hundreds of examples of TeleSeminars for you to browse, attend, model and evolve. Find the very latest by going to Google and searching for TeleSeminars and TeleClasses or check out your favorite coach training organization.

Here's just one that's met with a great deal of success.

It's an 8-week Tele-coaching seminar series that walks you through finding your ultimate profession, created by multiple streams maven Deborah Brown-Volkman.

Deborah charges $49 per person for the recording of this class. Check out Deborah's model at her site: http://www.surpassyourdreams.com/tele-coaching.html

Remember, some really worthy long-standing organizations have been built on the back of the almighty TeleSeminar, so put your mind to it. Like tofu, there's really very little you can't do with a Tele-Seminar, except maybe paint the ceiling of the Sistine Chapel.

How can you fit TeleSeminars into your Money Game Plan for Multiple Streams of Coaching Income?

Conversation Points

To offer at least one TeleSeminar in the next 30 days, what tools, systems or information do you need? Make a list.

Now shortlist and decide on a one-hour TeleSeminar topic. Determine the goal of your TeleSeminar. Is it to practice some new material? Sell a product? Get signups for an event?

Coaching Programs in a Box

Now that you've learned how to create your own TeleSeminars, here is an alternative that may interest coaches who'd rather not do the creating part.

Coaching Programs in a Box are complete turnkey coaching programs that Coaches like you can purchase. They are complete in terms of the program itself, instructor materials, and also include sales copy that you'll need in order to bring in more clients more profit.

Think of it as a short cut. If you can find a Program in a Box that suits your Niche market, you could be a small investment and very short day away from selling something new at your site.

Sample Program Titles include:

- 'Balancing Between Work and Life' for People Doing the 9-5 life
- Are You Cut Out to Run Your Business?
- Using Assessments To Help You Manage Your Team

- Marketing
- How to Make More Money in Less Time, for small business owners
- Rapid Relationship Recovery
- Succeeding as a Real Estate Agent
- Multiple Streams of Income for Single Moms
- Financial Freedom for Women

These 'in-a-box' programs allow you to offer your clients something tangible, with a clearly demarcated beginning, middle and end. It's the quickest way to 'product-ize' your services if you have some money to invest.

When choosing a Coaching Program in a Box, be sure to use the following criteria:

It's essential that there be a limited number of licenses offered.

If every other coach has the same program, the license isn't worth much. Inquire as to how many licenses are available and be sure to niche market your program so you distinguish yourself even further.

Look for a clear and thorough facilitator's guide.

A truly great licensed product comes with instructions. You wouldn't buy a McDonald's franchise without the Owner's Manual right?

Same goes here.

If possible, inquire about whether the program has been tested in the market. The demand for your program will depend on the topic. A little due diligence will go a long way.

Remember, offer a program your niche market wants, not what you want!

For a sample of some Coaching Programs in a Box go to:
http://www.msoci.com/cpib

If you know of others who are offering Coaching Programs in a Box, be sure to let me know.

Conversation Points

Which would you prefer, creating your own program, or purchasing a license for one? What are the pros and cons?

If you could have Programs in a Box on any topic, what topics would fit perfectly for your chosen Niche Market?

Companion Coaching Programs

Information Fatigue Syndrome n.
(def.) The weariness and stress that result from having to deal with excessive amounts of information. Also: IFS.

In a report done by Reuters News Agency, called 'Dying for Information?' 1,300 managers were surveyed in the U.S., Britain, Australia, Singapore and Hong Kong.

It was found that information anxiety is now a part of most executives' lives, leading to a new medical diagnosis, "information fatigue syndrome."

Survey results showed:

- 49% are unable to keep up with information flow
- 43% have trouble making important decisions because of data overload
- 38% waste substantial amount of valuable time trying to locate needed information

- 33% suffer from stress-related health problems brought on by too much information

And although the term Information Fatigue Syndrome is unlikely to find a home in the medical textbooks soon, personal and anecdotal evidence among coaches certainly validates this as a new social condition that affects nearly all of us.

What does this mean for Multiple Streams Coaches?

A lot of opportunity.

As I write this, I'm staring at a copy of Melissa Everett's very important book *"Making a Living While Making a Difference."*

I have at least five other books within reach, and a bookshelf of my favorite friends directly behind where I sit and type.

The premise of Companion Coaching Programs is that for every piece of popular intellectual property, there is an opportunity for greater learning to occur in a coaching setting. That setting then allows participants to implement to a greater degree new knowledge into their daily lives.

This isn't limited to print books however.

As discussed in another chapter, live trainings, especially bonanza 3-day conferences and the like, would also benefit from a Companion Coaching Program, as would literally any other significant piece of information or even systems and software for that matter.

Have a look at some of the most popular self-help books out there now.

Robert Kiyosaki's "Rich Dad, Poor Dad" now has a companion-coaching program to help his readers integrate his wisdom into real results. So does Michael Gerber's "E-myth." Even Tony Robbins has a telephone-based coaching program to support participants in his events.

How many great books now have this kind of coaching offering as a supplement?

A few, right?

Well let me ask you this: How many MORE transformational materials do NOT yet have a coaching component?

You got it.

Set this book down and take a look at your own bookshelf now and consider the possibilities.

Much like Oprah's Book Club selections form the basis of discussion, debate, reflection, and personal growth, Companion Coaching Programs can be delivered quickly to good effect by Multiple Streams Coaches such as you.

Have you noticed how many small new businesses and services are being created on a similar idea?

There are a growing number of businesses that have become so sophisticated that getting the most out of the service requires help from specialists like coaches.

Using Pay-Per-Click techniques has become essential to any online business owners success. The trouble is, just understanding the inside track at Google has become something of a maze.

Enter internet marketer Perry Marshall who has built several highly profitable streams of coaching income to help Google customers use Google better.

> *"This is going to be a lot more fun now that I understand Google a little bit better. Today - 50 clicks and 7.4% Click Thru Rate. On one promotion I took it from 1.1% all the way up to 4.5%.*
> -Kevin Thompson, Get Mold Solutions, Marysville, WA

You ask why isn't Google getting this kind of feedback?

If you said, "Because Google isn't in the business of using a coaching approach," you'd be right.

A coaching approach in the form of a Companion Coaching Program such as Perry's is going to 'win' in the eyes of the consumer every time.

Oh and about those consumers? Well, by conservative estimation, Perry's coaching groups and e-books on the topic of Google have impacted thousands of online businesses with increased productivity and profits.

And although Google doesn't officially sanction Perry's work, it certainly benefits massively from it in the form of more sales and exposure, so it's a definite three-way win.

Got any ideas yet, for your own Companion Coaching Program?

How about designing one for a live event?

What was the last conference or evening workshop you attended?

Did you apply everything you wanted to apply from what you learned there, intensively over several hours or days?

How much value would you put on a post-conference coaching program, specially priced to be affordable to attendees?

A follow-through program such as this would take the 'glow from the show' as it were, and take theory into action in a long lasting way.

The truth is, with all the information around us, there is so much that goes to waste. It's like massive information spillage, that a Multiple Streams coach with a strong Companion Coaching Program can help contain.

Take Coach to the Stars Ramon Williamson for example. He's the inventor of the concept "Your Official Conference Coach." What's that all about? Let's let Ramon's own words tell the story:

"Recently I spoke at Willie Crawford's Internet Marketing Weekend and instead of "pitching" my products; I decided to issue an unusual challenge:

"Over the next 12 days I will coach you to find a niche, create a product and launch it online using what you've learned here."

This is the kind of extreme, results-oriented coaching program that is my signature.

What happened?

Four people signed on and are completing the program."

As Official Conference Coach, Ramon turned what was simple conference 'information' into real results, real online products and revenue, by answering questions, building a supportive environment and of course lovingly kicking-butt in a coach-like way all the way along.

This successful Conference Companion Program is a model for many more to come.

It's a great way to take your coaching business to the next level quickly because:

- It will likely take you less time to create a companion product than to create one from scratch.
- You develop a brand very quickly as the "Google Adwords" Coach or the "Official Conference Coach."
- You can leverage the success of the business you are supporting, to reach existing customers who may be frustrated and turn them into fans of you and the product.
- You create residual exposure and revenue for the developers of the original intellectual property which eventually can lead to official joint venture relationships that lead to an even bigger leap for you.

Note too, that the format of your Companion Coaching Program can be one of many.

From multimedia video products teaching how to use software programs, eCourses on Napoleon Hill's classic titles, memberships that help 'land' the material delivered at Conferences or e-books and one-onone coaching sessions on Google AdWords...these are all ways in which Multiple Streams coaches can piggyback and get farther faster.

Facing facts, there is just so much intellectual property already in existence. And there are just so many people who struggle with information overload.

Both are compelling reasons to consider creating smart Companion Coaching Programs.

It's just a question of where to start.

Use the worksheet on the following page to get brainstorming. The first coaches to pull the trigger in each of the areas of potential will put themselves on a fast track to both revenue, and...reach far more clients with the precise help they seek in a lot less time.

Conversation Points

This is a particularly in-depth conversational section, because Companion Coaching Programs are a truly untapped realm. Take some time to deepen this conversation with your colleagues. It's the source of several weeks of valuable discussion.

What materials – books, articles or websites have you found most useful to your growth? List the titles and key points here:

What less orthodox materials have piqued your interest of late? For example, what is your favorite movie with a message?

On my to-do list is to create a Companion Coaching Program about environmental awareness that will be marketed to movie-goers and fans of such films as 'Erin Brockovich,' 'Soylent Green,' or 'The Day After Tomorrow.'

These movies are great examples of intellectual property that create the emotional energy to do something for the planet, but provide no direction on how to go about it.

What experts do you know – or could seek out – who have expertise you can bring to greater numbers by interviewing for audio or e-book, and who would benefit from added exposure?

(Who do you know who solves a problem a group of people have?)

Using the following as a real-life model, this is a particularly good exercise to tackle with your Multiple Streams Conversation partners.

The print book created by Web Wonder Coach Lynne Klippel is an outstanding example. It's a classic demonstration of an information product that was created using the Companion Coaching Program philosophy.

Lynne's expertise in this case was 12 Solopreneur Women, each with years of experience building business success online, yes, including yours truly. By packaging this collective wisdom into a book and CD set 'Web Wonder Women," Lynne harnessed existing intellectual property and gave it new packaging.

In doing so, Lynne will be able to provide coaching via book and audio to literally thousands of individuals. Find out more information about this treasure of a package at www.WebWonderWomen.com.

What pieces of technology – software or online services – have you worked hard to understand and use? Which ones have you let languish unused because you haven't made the effort to learn them?

What successful face-to-face or TeleSeminar based trainings are you currently offering that could have a Companion Coaching Program added to good effect? Think of this as a follow-through program.

What live trainings are you attending as a trainee or speaker that you could propose a Companion Coaching Program to?

Now brainstorm support programs for the above intellectual property.

The key is to take the existing knowledge, and translate it into real results.

Go through the above and mark the top three ideas with a 1, 2, 3 in the margin.

Now choose one and start into program planning...this can be sophisticated with multiple parts or more than likely quite simple, by using the intellectual property as a basis for study. Use your coaching know-how, tools, training ideas and more.

Coaching
Day Jobs

What do I mean by a 'Coaching Day Job?'

I have a pet theory about why bad things happen to good people. Or more specifically why tough times fall on coaches.

You know how they say you can't be a good writer if you haven't had some kind of angst in your life?

Or how it's one of those 'sad but true' things that comedians generally lead miserable lives and most of them smoke?

Well I have a theory about coaches who can't make money and it's quite simple.

My theory is that the coach really needs to go out right now and get themselves a day job.

Do you know Ken Wilber? Yes, author of numerous big books in the spiritual evolution arena, including *"A Theory of Everything"* and others?

Apparently he worked in a restaurant for 10 years washing dishes while writing those books.

And have you heard about Socrates, the ancient Greek philosopher and possibly the world's very first coach?

When he wasn't refining the art of a rhetorical question, he punched time as a stonemason.

The important thing here is not so much that these leaders 'had to work too', it's that they worked in a way that was in keeping with their greater calling.

Too often, I think, coaches think that taking a day job means that they are giving up coaching. Instead, I think it's something else rather simple: they are collecting important data, experience and wisdom they need to coach well.

If you're building a house by hand in the woods, you need to forage for materials before you can begin. And when a coach gets particularly stuck building his business, getting a day job is like putting on a big sack and heading out to collect materials.

So now when I'm coaching a coach who just can't seem to make the shifts or decisions that move them from playing to earning a living as a coach, I've made a practice of asking them if they're willing to do a 'Castanza'.

What's a 'Castanza'? Well you should ask!

Most of you will be familiar with the television sitcom, 'Seinfeld'. One of Jerry Seinfeld's friends was a character named George Castanza.

George was one of these people who couldn't do anything right. In his thirties, he lived at home, had no job, no relationship, was balding, short and generally unattractive. He put it like this:

George: It's not working, Jerry. It's just not working.

Jerry: What is it that isn't working?

George: Why did it all turn out like this for me? I had so much promise. I was personable, I was bright. Oh, maybe not academically speaking, but ... I was perceptive. I always know when someone's uncomfortable at a party. It became very clear to me sitting out there today, that every decision I've ever made, in my entire life, has been wrong. My life is the opposite of everything I want it to be. Every instinct I have, in every life, be it something to wear, something to eat ... It's all been wrong.

But one day, in one of the episodes, George had an epiphany that to me was a brilliant coaching moment. (You see, coaching is all around us.)

He decided, in all his frustration, to do everything the 'opposite' which of course leads to some great things happening pretty much straight away.

When things just aren't working in your practice-building efforts, consider whether doing just the opposite of what you think should work...might actually work.

Take a day job much like a reporter doing a story would pretend to be a 'lady of the evening' for research.

Wherever you land, do your job, take heart, and as you acknowledge the human beings all around you, be a coach. Practice coaching. It doesn't matter if you're delivering pizza, you can do it with a coaching approach.

It doesn't matter if you spend time in the boardroom, you can observe proceedings with a coaching eye.

What better test of your intent to help others live better lives, than to walk a mile in their shoes and find joy?

How would a coach driving a taxi for a living drive it differently than someone else?

How would an administrative assistant approach a cranky boss?

How would a lawn care professional, chiropractor, doggie daycare owner, hairdresser of cell phone salesman?

We all know the difference between a regular person doing time in their job and someone taking a coaching approach. It's obvious and immediate when you see it.

Director of Consulting Services for a Fortune 50 Company, Coach Lable Braun is a terrific example. I'll let him tell you in his own words:

> "I consider myself a coach with an income in excess of six figures who doesn't have a single client.
>
> In my job, that I am paid very well for, I use little else than my coaching skills. In fact, in the Project Coaching presentation I did for the New York City Midtown Coaching Center, I said that one of the main objectives of Project Coaching was to make "Coach" a job code

in the HR system of every Fortune 500 company, just like "Database Analyst" is a job code, and "Engineer" is a job code, and "CEO" is a job code.

I thought the coaches would revolt at the idea of being job codes in the corporate environment. Instead, they loved it!

Andrea, there are so many people out there who make wonderful coaches, but just don't have it in them to be entrepreneurs. We can't leave them behind.

We have to create an environment in the corporate world where there can be a job code tied to a regular paycheck, doing their wonderful coaching."

Until the day comes when you can get hired as a coach within any company in the Yellow Pages, consider the benefits of some added life experience by taking a regular day job of some sort.

By taking a coaching approach to a day job, you'll help make the case for a Job Code too.

As I complete this book, I've been mentally reviewing whether or not my next book should be 'How to Be An Almost-Perfect Wife, A Coaching Approach to Love.'

If so, I'm quite sure that I'll be taking time, taking a day job, and doing some interesting living first.

For the veteran coaches who've been at it since the early days, could it be that it's time to get back in the field for a spell?

For those of you on the fence, would doing some 'real work' help sharpen your senses for your time with coaching clients?

What do you think the impact would be on your current coaching clients if you added a Stream of Coaching Income that on the outside looked like a paycheck?

Write to me about it. I'll put your correspondence in the 'Undercover Coach' file...and your data will inform the rest of us.

Now please, this is important.

If you are a coach hanging on with serious financial difficulties, you know who you are.

Consider getting a Coaching Day Job very seriously.

It's not a betrayal of your dreams.

Consider taking a day job that releases you from financial strain and then show up for each shift as you are now, a coach.

While doing this, keep reading this book and honing your coaching skills. Most of all, observe, listen, question and relate...all within the context of your day job.

> *"For God does not send us despair in order to kill us; he sends it in order to awaken us to new life."*
> Herman Hesse

More information about the ongoing project of creating tools and resources, support and guidance for coaches looking for great Coaching Day Jobs is available at **www.CoachingDayJobs.com** You are NOT alone.

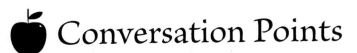 # Conversation Points

Do you think a person can take a Day Job and still be a coach?

What do you think of the movement to create a Job Code for coaches in corporations? What are you willing to do to support this development?

If you are struggling financially, could it be that taking a Day Job is the most responsible thing you can do for your current and potential one-on-one clients?

By relieving your financial strain, you can be clear-headed for your clients, now and later.

Who do you know that you can share this concept with? A colleague who is trying to make ends meet? How can you best share the idea that a Coaching Day Job could be what they need?

Affiliate Programs

Are you having trouble creating new product offerings from scratch? Maybe you're not a natural writer or you're unsure of a topic? Or maybe you'd just like a shortcut to some reliable revenue?

Not to worry, help is here.

And even if you're not stuck creating your own intellectual property, the concept of promoting other people's products and earning coaching income is an idea whose time is fast on its way.

Selling other people's products, and earning a percentage of the sales price for your efforts is what's referred to online as earning money as an 'affiliate.'

Within the next 12 months, the internet is getting set to see a significant number of coaches begin to grow their one-on-one practices with the help of someone else's products.

In fact, it promises to be a big trend, and I hope you're one of the first.

Multiple Streams Coach Natalie Miller of AskNatalie.net is a great example. Her latest offering is called "*The Un-Parenting Crusade*" and her first self-created product is a 15-part eCourse on the 15 Parenting Paradigms.

When asked, "Is the eCourse going to be for pay, Natalie?"

Her reply was, "No, it will be my free offering at the top of my Product Funnel, but I have some great affiliate products that I will embed into the eCourse and generate some revenue that way." Super stuff.

In this way, every time one of Natalie's eCourse readers decide to purchase one of the affiliate products she recommends, Natalie will receive a small commission.

Since she plans to subscribe hundreds if not thousands of parents to her Un-Parenting eCourse, the number of people who will take a look at her recommended products will not be insignificant, and Natalie's Affiliate income will continue to increase.

The fact is, through Natalie's promotional efforts, parents around the world will be exposed to a great product that she personally recommends, and their parenting will be better for it.

"How fortunate we are to have Natalie Miller on board for the Nurturing Parent Program! She has a knack for relating to every personality and issue that may arise."
Stephanie Murray, Prevent Child Abuse Vermont

Over the course of months and years, this means hundreds of parents and their families impacted.

You can bet that with each relationship she builds, each new affiliate program she adds and recommends will mean more revenue for her, more families impacted, and more revenue for the creator of the product too.

All at relatively little added effort to Natalie.

In fact, the very best coach affiliates will do some work. That is, they'll create some content that bridges the gap between the audience and the product, rather than simply saying "Hey, buy this."

That's where the coaching approach comes in.

In Natalie's case, each of the 15-eCourse lessons will be about a new parenting paradigm. By talking about the new paradigm, opening dialog and fielding questions, Natalie sets the stage for her affiliate products.

Her readers will naturally see how purchasing additional items will help them achieve greater shifts in their parenting.

This turns knowledge of the 15 paradigms into action - the act of integrating additional products. A perfect example of Natalie fulfilling a coaching role, even though the product isn't her own.

So...do you have a product that you especially favor? Do you feel strongly that more people could benefit from knowing about it?

Because the coaches who are readers of my personal blog at AndreaJLee.com are predisposed to embrace the fact that when I recommend something, it's for real, each time I do so means added revenues of several hundred within a few days.

I choose the recommended items very carefully. It's my way of living up to the trust placed in me.

That's what promoting affiliate programs are all about folks, really. That is, if you're a coach and understand the coaching approach.

At a very basic level, you can also simply add Google AdSense ads to your website. These add revenue just by being clicked by people at your site. These are more of a numbers game but it helps if you make sure your website content matches your ads.

To take it further, perhaps you've personally experienced half a dozen products that have changed your life in some way, be those books, CDs or some kind of training.

If so, what can you do to demonstrate to those around you the power of that offering?

And what will it mean to the creator of that offering, to have your support promoting it?

There are two key things to know about selecting affiliate programs to support:

1. Give more than a simple recommendation. Use this opportunity to write an article, create a 3-page website, compile a PDF report, or even tape a brief audio about why your audience should sit up and notice this product.

Speak from the heart about the difference it has made to you. Tell a story. Ask questions that engage the reader. All of these are techniques exemplifying a coaching approach.

Then embed the links for your recommendations within the body of your article.

In this way, you add value, and you're much more likely to create a connection that leads to real impact, and a purchase that leads to earnings for you.

2. Especially if you are having difficulty choosing a niche market for your own practice, hunting for worthwhile affiliate programs can be a great exercise.

Other people's work that deserves to reach more people can benefit from your energy and as you earn money through affiliate programs, you'll learn a great deal about what sparks your passion.

At the same time, by making an integrity-based recommendation, you strengthen your bond with your readers in a way that always results in more revenue in your other streams.

You know how when you buy something from a certain brand that you end up liking, you go back and buy more of that brand?

Same thing. As your audience comes to trust your recommendations, they're more and more likely to purchase other things from you.

Win, win, & win.

As a Multiple Streams Coach, you've put yourself on a path to becoming great at both creating products AND marketing them.

As we've seen throughout the book with some terrific examples, coaches are uniquely suited to bringing these two skill sets together in a way that adds up to more than a lifetime of income.

As you travel along the learning path, there's no reason not to go forth and find people who have created fantastic products and can benefit from your ability to spread the word.

Armed with a coaching approach, your growing marketing savvy will be a blessing to them and bring you added income. Hey, it's the Multiple Streams way, baby!

There are literally thousands of people promoting affiliate programs on the Internet. But the coaches that take a coaching approach to this opportunity are the ones who'll go to the top of the class.

People don't like to be told to buy something without understanding why, and believing that you have their best interests at heart. So have a look at just a couple additional examples of great affiliate promotions and see what you can see.

Besides, if you don't, all those pesky internet marketers who don't know squat what it means to be a coach will continue raking in the cash promoting affiliate programs to virtual strangers.

Eek!! Go on, get going...

Conversation Points

Which products at Clickbank.com or CJ.com are of interest to you? Shortlist a dozen or so and purchase one or two that you can personally benefit from right now. If you can recommend it, do so to your existing subscriber base using an affiliate link.

Coaching
Gyms

Just what is a Coaching Gym?

There are a lot of different variations of the Coaching Gym concept, but there is at least one common element that usually makes a Coaching Gym a Coaching Gym.

Instead of coaching clients one-on-one each week at an appointed day and time, the Coaching Gym is set up so that certain days and hours of the week are designated for open coaching.

Clients can call or 'drop in' to the gym when and if they wish, and access coaching.

The client calls are still one-on-one, but they can be very short, say 5, 10 or 15 minutes or longer if necessary.

And because not every client in the Gym will call each week, there is usually room for more clients in your business. And therein lays the leverage points.

From the Multiple Streams point of view, a Coaching Gym allows you to serve more clients superlatively within less time. You don't have to sit at your desk and wait for the phone to ring one hour after the next, one client after another.

Because you can handle a larger number of clients obviously means increased revenue, and the extra time gives you the ability to build other streams of revenue should you wish.

The absolute best example of an existing Coaching Gym is the one that Million Dollar Coach Chris Barrow has built within the dentistry niche. Chris used to be a client of OnlineBusinessManager.com for companies wishing to accelerate their growth from six figures to seven.

Using this Gym model, he built a coaching practice supporting dentists that continues to be in the seven figures.

Here a portion of a recent interview with Chris:

How many clients are in the Dentist's Coaching Gym Chris?

At the moment, about 140 clients, each paying approx. US$500/month.

What does the Dentist's Coaching Gym consist of?

Quarterly live workshops focused on 8 Key Strategies. Email and Telephone access for laser coaching on a weekly basis. Print and electronic resource documents and customer support from the Dentist's Coaching Gym Customer Support Manager.

How many emails do you receive a day?
At the moment, about 15/20 a day from 140 clients.

How many calls a day?

At the moment, about 6 a day from 140 clients.

Do they all use the gym, Chris?

No – just like a real gym, I have a few fanatics, about 20% very regular attendees, 20% who pay and never show up and the rest who call in periodically, when the fancy takes them;

Does anyone complain or ask for a refund?

No –it has never happened because the rules are spelled out, just as you have read them, before they start in the Gym.

Do you always answer the phone?

Mostly, yes, but if I'm working on a project that requires some peace and solitude, then I will let the voice mail collect messages until I am though – I'm in a meeting with me!

Is there a common theme to the gym visits?

You bet there is – problems with staff, problems with money, problems with patient communication, self-doubt, 'how do I do this?' questions.

For the latter, I collect my replies into articles for magazines, post some of them on my web site and either send copies to clients if a question is repeated or point them at the download – over time you can build a pretty good library of answers.

Did clients who transitioned from one-on-one to gym grumble?

Yes they did. After they had finished grumbling they just got on with it.

How long do the coaching calls last?

Average I would say is 15 minutes. Occasionally, I will spend longer if there is a real challenge in the call but most often the calls are swift and to the point.

A favorite technique of mine is to ask the client to separate the situation from the way they feel about the situation. I then ask them if they want to be coached on the situation or on their feelings.

Overwhelmingly, they will respond that it's the situation that they want help with. Very effective.

What do the clients think?

They love it – that's because marketing is the process by which you eliminate the clients that you do not want to work with. Provided the Coaching Gym concept is spelled out very clearly before you begin, the clients who don't like it, don't hire you. In the words of that great philosopher Hannibal Lecter – "goody, goody."

> *"We now have complete financial control of the business - a fantastic support team, and a plan for the future. On a personal level my net income has increased, I have reduced my hours considerably, increased my holidays and I have much more time away from the business to spend with my family. Employing*

Chris as your business coach will be the best business decision you will make."
-Dr Anthony Fagg BDS – Staffordshire

In conclusion, I'm gusting up to 185 clients this year [2003], a million dollars in gross revenues, lots of profit, lots of time off, a great adventure of a life – and, most important of all, a file of testimonial letters from my clients that tell me I make a real difference in their lives.

If you are currently coaching quite a few one-on-one clients and are looking for a way to shift to a multiple streams approach, consider modeling a Coaching Gym.

It's a lot like setting up 'teaching assistant' hours within a college setting. Students show up when they need help, and don't when they don't need help, or are just lazy. In between students showing up, you can work on your other streams!

For more help on building a Coaching Gym within a particular niche market... remember, the formula is Niche + Problem + Packaging (in this case the packaging is the Gym format)...consider Chris' mentoring program at **www.thecoachingbusinessschool.com** or **www.theCoachingGym.com**

After a great foundational year of helping coaches build Gyms for specialty markets, he is accepting a maximum of 50 Coaches who are committed to following his model as a franchise holder.

Hats off to Chris for beating a path for a future of profitable Coaching Gyms impacting thousands of clients around the globe.

Conversation Points

Having read this far in the Multiple Streams of Coaching Income book, what is your idea of a perfect coaching business? Name three criteria.

If you switched to a Coaching Gym model, you would likely free up at least 10-20% of your time each week. What could you use that time towards?

Coaching
Prime Time

An awful lot of fantastic coaching has been coming out of Hollywood lately, have you noticed?

Whether it's Morgan Spurlock's feature film debut *"Super size Me"...*

"Michael Moore's *"Fahrenheit 9/11"* also on the big screen...

Or the immense coaching breakthrough moments in *"Queer Eye for the Straight Guy"...*

Tears of joy and newfound confidence in *"What Not to Wear"...*

And ABC's life changing *"Extreme Makeover, Home Edition"...*

It's undeniable. Coaching has come, and found its place in what I consider to be some of the very best work coming out of Hollywood.

And that's not even mentioning the more obvious *"Starting Over"* and other reality TV shows that revolve around the idea of changing lives for the better through Life Coaching.

Pretty darned cool stuff especially when you consider the limitless reach of television and film in our lives. Will video games with a coaching theme be next? Well if those things have to exist, I can only hope.

Question for you.

Seeing as we're talking about movies and such.

If you were the last coach on earth, and it was up to you to save the world from its impending doom, who would be the 10 people you would do ANYTHING to coach.

In other words, if your coaching skills were the only thing between survival and certain death and destruction, what 10 people would you choose, out of all the people you know, or maybe who you currently coaching, to coach like a fiend, and save the day?

I know it's a pretty funny premise. And no, I don't think any studios will come a-knocking, but I do have a reason for asking.

I strongly believe that coaching has a large role to grow into, to coach those in the public eye, whether that be actors, directors, studio executives, station owners, news programmers, journalists, politicians at all levels of government.

In fact, I'll call it a responsibility of the coaching profession going forward.

These are the people who, through coaching, can be said to have a level of influence that has the potential to spread the effects of coaching to the Nth degree.

Don't get me wrong, there is nothing small or unworthy about coaching clients who aren't in the public arena.

But it was Archimedes who said *"Give me a lever long enough and I will move the world."*

If we consider that the local television or newspaper news is consumed by millions of people around the world, and that decisions about what story 'leads' or what 'angle' is taken usually fall to just a few individuals in each city...

We start to realize that coaching prime time figures has truly untapped potential to change the world. Dramatically.

I'm sad to say I've seen some terrible movies in my life. I kid you not; I've wished the director, the actors, the set designers who made all that 'blood' and other violent paraphernalia...I've wished just one of them had a coach.

If just 10,000 skilled coaches were to take on one high profile client, those would be results worth talking about.

Put it another way.

In the year I'm writing this, the reality television show *"Survivor"* has been on the air for 8 seasons.

After the finale where the million-dollar winner was declared, I posted a lengthy rant to my blog at AndreaJLee.com

It outlines what I continue to think to be an extraordinary opportunity for coaches.

It's worth sharing again here:

<begin blog posted May 10, 2004, title 'Survivor Coaching'>

Did you watch the 3-hour long finale of *Survivor* last night?

I did. (Whew.)

And as usual (it's an illness, I know)... seeing the veritable train wreck of emotions and corresponding potential for greatness in the 18 contestants...it made me think about coaching and life.

I know a few coaches (not many, but a few) who have chosen a sensational and high profile niche. They coach celebrities, or wannabe celebrities.

As you likely know, the survivor contestants are somewhere in between, and some would say a little stuck.

Do you know any survivor contestant who has parlayed their ten minutes of fame on the show into more than a commercial (Colby Donaldson and Gillette Razors), a radio show and occasional spot on entertainment show TV (Richard Hatch) or the obligatory Playboy spread? (Jeri Manthey, Jenna Morascia, winner Amber Brkich pictured above, others.)

Anyone?

Hmm. Out of the 9 Survivor shows in total, 18 contestants each, that's a whopping 162 people, am I right? All in the Survivor Alum Club.

Arguably many of these individuals did it just for the fun of it. But certainly as the years have gone by, reality shows have become one way for regular folk to get a toehold into Hollywood.

And yet more than a toehold seems to elude 99%, even if you consider *Big Brother, The Apprentice or The Mole, Bachelor*, etc. etc.

Could it be the survivors of these programs are prime candidates for...a coach?

One that can help them wind their way through the jungle to something lasting and fulfilling?

One that can steer them from the weedy murk of a terrible public indictment such as the one the aforementioned Jeri received last night? (Cast on both Survivor shows she was on as the "witchy one" she was booed by 5000 audience members last night before she even opened her mouth, and ended up leaving the stage during a commercial, very upset.)

Eek, that seems like a sure case for TherapyVille, before a coach, but that's beside the point.

Are you a Celebrity Coach? Are you picking up the phone and connecting with the 18 "newly-released-from-captivity" contestants, helping them see that -- without a coach who can be objective and talk them through the jungle that is Hollywood their chances of really making it big, and taking advantage of their momentary 'IT' factor, are slim?

The potential for greatness emanating off these folks is palpable. Overachievers all. Savvy in the eye of the camera, well spoken, attractive even under the ugliest of conditions sans toothpaste, soap and everything.

Whether that potential is realized though, I dunno, will that be luck, hard work on their part, or maybe a little help from someone...you?

It occurs to me that there are hundreds of people in the public eye who could be ideal clients for any number of us. We can literally see where they could benefit from coaching, before even approaching them.

How compelling would it be for any contestant to receive a personal call saying,

"Hey Rob, congratulations on your engagement. Have you thought about how you're going to capitalize on your success on the show, rehabilitate your image in the eye of the public, and let the world know you're not a liar who'll do anything for money?

And then go on to make sure you live life happily ever after?

Well, what I do is...."

Calling all celebrity Coaches and Survivors for comment.

And please? If you saw the show last night, you know what

I mean. With the utmost of love and respect, please, please, someone get Jeri to a therapist, fast. Jeri, I have high hopes for you. I just hope you're open to receiving help.

As for the rest of the contestants...I guess its open season for the coach that gets through to them first.

Let me know how you do with proficiency #3, okay?

<end blog post>

The real beauty of taking up the challenge of Coaching Prime Time is that you already know a great deal about the client, where they're coming from, and where they possibly would like to go.

Not only does that mean you have an unparalleled opportunity to coach from strength, but you also have fantastic leverage from which to 'pitch' your coaching services.

It's a classic example of being able to 'listen' to your clients week after week, to understand them, and then make them a coaching offer they can't refuse.

Oh and of course, a side benefit? Succeed with just one prime time client, and your viral word of mouth hits the roof.

Fantastic, motivated, paying clients, the ability to impact large numbers of people through your work, and a little bit of monster marketing as a byproduct.

It doesn't get much better than that, does it?

Be sure to send tickets to the Oscars!

Conversation Points

Name three people in Hollywood, public office or otherwise in the public eye that you would like to coach. Why would you like to coach them and how do you think it would be best to reach them to start?

Although you may not watch a lot of television, how can you use popular culture to help you be a better coach to your clients? In what ways can you leverage the entertainment industry to your benefit in your coaching sessions or in the products in your Product Funnel?

If you're interested in learning more about the wave of spirituality as it gains momentum in Hollywood and other centers of entertainment, you may find it invigorating to support the "*The Spiritual Cinema Circle*" which focuses on spiritual movies and films.

Launched in April 2004, by Stephen Simon (Producer and Director of "What Dreams May Come" (with Robin Williams), and "Somewhere in Time" (with Christopher Reeve and Jane Seymour) this is a subscription based service that will send you new spiritual movies each month.

Find out more at www.SpiritualCinemaCircle.com.

It's one of many ways you and your clients can start building an environment that inspires and uplifts you. Who would you enjoy sharing the *Spiritual Cinema Circle* with?

We are what we eat, yes, and that includes food for our hearts, minds and souls.

Multimedia Coaching

A book on Multiple Streams of Coaching Income would be remiss without a chapter on advanced technology.

The truth is the dream of coaching by hologram is likely not too far off. I predict I will see at least a prototype within the next ten years.

But you don't have to wait that long to get started building some of the more technical streams of coaching income.

Let's start with some of the multimedia some creative coaches are already using to make their clients sit up and take note.

Just a short year or so ago, talk of producing a video ezine would bring on shrieks of 'too difficult,' 'too much bandwidth,' etc.

With the advent of desktop video software, it's a reality.

Go to this link for an example of an ezine that contains video (near the bottom.)

www.7dayebook.com/the-Biggest-Lie-Ever-Told.html

This kind of desktop video is becoming more popular, and is definitely worth considering if you have materials your clients would like to 'see' you deliver.

The software allows you to record your actions on your own computer. You can edit, paste, crop, and do all sorts of nifty things, foremost of which is of course, post a copy of the video clip at your website.
This kind of show-me-how format can be great for critiquing websites, demonstrating how to use software, or any number of other things.

Because it's accompanied by your recorded voice, you can literally coach the client through the steps of how to do something. Maybe you're a wealth coach. You could use desktop video to demonstrate how to read the stock pages at an online newspaper website.

And Un-Marketing Coach Scott Stratten made his video go supersonic at **www.scottstratten.com/movie.html** Check Scott's site out for an outstanding example of a coaching approach followed by an invitation to subscribe to his ezine.

The tools it takes to make this type of video happen aren't hard to master; most people just don't go to the bother to try it. To give it a whirl, download just the trial for now, at **www.Camtasia.com**

Other uses of video for Multiple Streams Coaches include traditional video for television, on VCR or DVD format.

The quickest way to creating a video product is to hold a local workshop and record it for video and audio.

Whether there are many or few in your audience is close to irrelevant; your greater purpose here is to create a sellable video product for those who don't live near you.

Planned right, you can find economical videographers who'll discount their prices outside of wedding season, and away you go.

To see a great example of a video product created in this very manner, check out the ClownMarketingTips.com website which belongs to Business Coach Esther Beris.
Another Coach doing some work in the area of Webinars is Mentor Coach Alicia Smith.

She is presenting a DiSCNinja.com Webinar with PictureTalk where her audience will be 50-100 employees and managers from High Technology, Financial, Healthcare/Pharmaceutical Companies, Education and Government Agencies.

Afterward, she'll have a recorded version of her webinar available for sale for those who couldn't attend live. Voila, Alicia's reward for being on the leading edge? Another compelling income stream.

What is a Webinar?

Live Webinars are rapidly becoming the next generation of information delivery and an important technology to consider for Multiple Streams Coaching.

Webinars use a system that usually requires no special software. Your clients can participate in a live on-line seminar utilizing just a computer, telephone, and Internet connection.

As the Webinar host, you will be able to present materials in real-time, talking and showing materials simultaneously.

Particularly if you service the corporate market, you'll find this technology is being very well received, but webinars are also great for live demonstrations of technology and so on, so coaches working with small business owners may be great candidates too.

Now that you can show things to your clients as if you were actually there, no more fumbling around trying to describe a visual concept. It's a great, exciting enhancement of coaching services as we know them.
As several of the Multiple Streams members remarked, using many different multimedia methods of delivering coaching services can really be impressive.

"It's great getting tidbits of coaching in all these different formats. It's like you're everywhere! I can't get away from your encouragement around here; I guess I have to just get my streams done."

I had to chuckle because it's the exact effect I had hoped for.

With a teleseminar each month, email coaching, audio clips, desktop video, and even the occasional item by mail, it's a 'You're surrounded!' approach to coaching that helps.

As we so often say, our environment really helps support us in our goals, and using multimedia is the best way I know of to equip a coach to build a three-dimensional environment for their clients.

A case in point is a new technology called Direct-To-Desktop.

It's an alternate to email delivery for text-based materials, and about half the current Multiple Streams members are using it.

Although the technology isn't yet perfect, it's very handy because it bypasses email and reduces the chances of the material getting filtered, deleted or just plain ignored.

Direct-to-Desktop technology requires a small download for the Coach, and another smaller download for each client. Once complete, this allows the Coach to send material direct to the client's desktop, by making a small icon 'flash' in the bottom right hand corner of the screen.

Material can be pre-scheduled so you can deliver it if you are away. And it keeps track of how many times it was opened, etc.

As you go about building your coaching business, you may find technology more frustrating than interesting.

It's true that the rate of new advancements can create a kind of future shock that isn't useful.

What I recommend you do is set aside some time to play with new things. I do so simply to stay ahead of those I'm mentoring so they don't have to worry about it.

Whatever new technology becomes important to coaches, you'll know because I'll fill you in.

That said, sometimes it's just fun to explore for yourself, so set aside one afternoon a month to experiment with new things. Call it 'playtime.'

And outside of that, don't let new technology phase you. Your focus needs to be on building the streams of income that will provide the most value to your niche market, that answer their specific problems, in the packaging that's most accessible to you.

With that, how about a little play time?

There are a few trends that you may want to start percolating on right now, because from what I can see, they can have a positive impact on the first coaches that embrace them.

SitePal.com is a site that allows you to create speaking animated characters for your web site, and add your own audio message too.

Similarly, you can converse with Audrey, the first ever chatterbot who is studying coaching under the guidance of Coach John Satta. Ask Audrey your hardest coaching question at **CoachingTechnology.com**

Can't think of how you'd use this technology? Browse around at **www.pandorabots.com/botmaster/en/mostactive** for some ideas.

In the next 90 or 180 days, you're bound to bump into new technology that can improve your coaching.

If your Product Funnel is well in hand, I encourage you to take advantage.

As with all new things, it's the people who take an early chance and dive in before the others do that will reap the financial rewards.

And if you aren't in a position to lead with new technology, make it your goal to position yourself close to people who do.

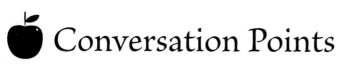 # Conversation Points

What is your attitude towards new technology? What approach do you take to synthesize new information about technology?

Brainstorm ways Desktop Video, Traditional Video, Direct-to-Desktop technology and animated characters could enhance your coaching business. Could some of this new technology help you as you build your product funnel?

What other new technology trends have you observed that can have an impact on your coaching business?

Chopping Wood, Carrying Water

The Nature of the Transition Facing Coaches

Welcome to the 'Chop Wood, Carry Water' portion of the book.

At this point, you're absorbing some of the fundamental mindset shifts I've invited you to make towards coaching.

- Coaching is not a profession, it's an approach.
- Successful coaches are not only coaches with 30 clients a week. Successful coaches embody coaching in an integrated way and use multiple avenues to bring the coaching approach to the world.
- There is no scarcity of opportunity to make an impact on the world through coaching. The world is waiting with increasing expectation for coaches to step up.
- There's a Coaching Solution to Every Problem.

You've also shaken up some of your thinking about what Marketing is.

- Great marketing is engaging people in conversations that result in their greater good. Not heavy-handed efforts at

separating them from their money.
- Great marketing goes deep with a specific segment of the population. Not surface attempts at getting the attention of billions.

By following the formula, Niche + Problems + Packaging = Coaching Income, you can avoid many of the biggest marketing pitfalls. And in the last section of the book, you've read about a variety of concrete ways to create real revenue streams for yourself.

There are additional ways to create streams of coaching income that we cover in a hands-on fashion at the Multiple Streams website, but you've now had a good look at quite a few.

Congratulations on reading this far, and being open to some of the paradigm shifts facing coaches today.

This is a good point in the book to make a special note.

As coaches, you are more aware than many, that paradigm shifts can take time to take root.

In fact, the deeper the shifts you are trying to make, the more uneasy the transition can feel.

We work as partners with clients to accelerate the times when they are growing into new identities, breaking out of old ways of looking at things, and generally rebirthing themselves.

Let's do the same with ourselves shall we?

If you're ready to jump headfirst into a new identity for yourself as a coach, that's fantastic.

Gleefully shedding limiting beliefs about what we can do, how we should do it, and what that should look like is, in a word, exciting!

And, sooner or later, a certain stickiness hits. Maybe it shows up as a feeling of being 'uncomfortable in your own skin.'
It's the nature of transitions.

So...how do you work through this?

Given that your desire and commitment to grow is steadfast, what can you do to avoid speed bumps, and accelerate your way to the next level of play?

That's what the 'Chop Wood, Carry Water' section of the book is about.

This section of the book outlines a handful of things that I hope will ease your journey to multiple streams.

As I've helped others through the transition, and as I go through it myself with each new personal growth phase, these are the things that seem to help.

You can't skip transitions, but there are ways to make them easier. Read on.

Conversation Points

How did you used to identify yourself as a Coach?

What are the three biggest shifts you are making around your identity as a coach as a result of the conversation we're having in the Multiple Streams of Coaching Income book?

What three positive and three negative things come up for you as you think about taking steps towards building real streams of coaching income over and above one-on-one coaching?

From One to Many

One of the first stumbling blocks new Multiple Streams Coaches face is the challenge of coaching a large number of people at once through writing, audio, speaking, etc.

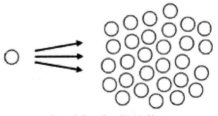

Figure 8: From One (You) to Many

As opposed to the old model of intimate conversations being held one-on-one on the telephone.

Even coaches who have arguably had the greatest of success coaching one-on-one can suddenly get a case of stage fright when it comes to recording their first interview for an Audio CD.

Big self-doubting questions sprout up.

- How do I say this in a way that all of these people will 'get' at once?
- How do I possibly bring value to such a large group?
- How can I relate to all of these people deeply all at once?

Somehow the advice that seemed so sound for one person feels a little limp when delivered too many.

This is a particular characteristic of the transition to becoming a Multiple Streams Coach.

At its essence, it's a simple issue of confidence, but the useful question here is often, "How can coaches build this confidence up?"

A few things:

- Visualize one person who represents your niche. Best if they are a real person you know. Create your product with them firmly in mind.
- Journal your one-on-one coaching sessions. Adapt each universal issue you address one-on-one into a product offering in one of the Multiple Streams formats.
- Engage directly with one person you feel represents a problem in your chosen niche. Interview them and record the ensuing interaction.

Voice-over artists, news anchors, and radio announcers are trained in much the same way. Even though it's called 'broadcasting,' when they get on the air, they actually practice 'narrowcasting.'

The person talking about the latest hamburger meal deal on the radio? They're picturing their best friend and talking right to them.

It's one of the best ways to get out of a stage-fright induced rut, along the road to multiple streams of income.

Conversation Points

What do you work on with one-on-one clients most frequently? If one person is going through it, many could benefit from your help.

How could you repackage your wisdom and expertise on this topic? What 'bottled' formats can you consider?

How can you practice transitioning from coaching one person at a time to many at a time?

Accelerating Your 'What'

Knowledge, skills and experience have been said to be the three things every coach brings to the table for a client.

While coaching skills are the most attended to of the three elements (coaching schools, training programs, seem to preoccupy the majority of coaches) the other two should not be overlooked.

What you bring (your experience) and what you know (your knowledge) can often have more bearing on the outcome of coaching than even coaching skills, although certainly they are helpful too.

So just what do I mean by the phrase "accelerating your 'what' " and why is it so important?

We talked in an earlier chapter about the importance of filtering information for our clients. And the fact that in future, the most valued coaches will be Human Googles for their clients.

What you know, and what you have lived through, is part of your filter. And whether you realize it or not, you have a lot to say about your filter – in fact, you can design your own, and consciously change it by adding to your knowledge.

My challenge to you is this. What are you doing on a daily basis to strengthen, inform, flex, and feed your brain?

What knowledge do you possess that affects how you filter for your clients? Better yet, what DON'T you know, that knowing... would help your clients?

As coaches, it's our responsibility to attend to the ongoing feeding of our 'what.'
When you read a book, does it affect your coaching?

When you experience something cathartic, does it change your coaching sessions?

What if instead of floating along the river of life, you proactively sought out experiences that would enrich yourself and your coaching clients?

If we are to guide our clients, influence our readers, inspire our relationships, accelerating our 'what' is a priority.

So, what company are you keeping that continually stimulates you? Who around you provides a regular intellectual spark that leads to sparkling late-night conversations? Whose book recommendations do you take?

One of my personal favorite rituals is reading. In fact, reading to me is a form of prayer or meditation.

The act of reading fertilizes, moisturizes and exercises my brain, and my clients benefit immeasurably.

Reading more than one book at a time can have an interesting effect. What results is a new and different combination of thoughts that is almost as good as having two authors in the room with you and creating a debate.

What would Tom Collins say to Tom Peters on that point I wonder? Oh, how interesting it would be to get Michael Gerber in here to rebut that!

Most recently I've wondered what would happen if I could bring 'Creating' author Robert Fritz and 'Structure is Destiny' author Dr. Joel Orr together for a conversation. Since I can't, I'm reading both their books at once.

With me as filter, you just don't know what might end up connecting!

I invite you to invite great conversations to take up a place of honor in your brain.

I invite you to create rich and unexpected conversations.

Lead yourself and your clients to unexplored creativity by committing to a personal practice of accelerating your 'what.'

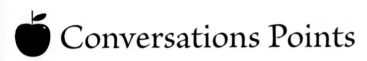

Conversations Points

What two books, magazines or speakers have piqued your interest of late?

How do the ideas of these two separate bodies of work combine? Do they build on each other, do they clash; where on the spectrum of opinion do you fit?

What are three topics that you know absolutely nothing about? And what will you do to find out more about them?

(For example, I am currently learning about body building, what it means and feels like to have a PhD degree, and interviewing smart people about what 'legacy' means to them.)

Taking notes as you read will help you integrate new thoughts more quickly. Also, it is a proven and reliable way to generate original intellectual property of your own.

When you next pick up something to read, record your thoughts and reactions in a notepad. In what ways can you use your notes to help build new products for your Product Funnel?

The Biz of Coaching

Let's get this stumbling block out of the way too, shall we?

For as long as I have worked with coaches, this issue has come been problematic.

Have you heard all the hullabaloo about how important it is for coaches to learn the business of running a coaching business?

Probably countless times right?

Alright, well, bear with me; I'm going to make this short and sweet.

It's true that along the path to becoming an outstanding Multiple Streams Coach, you will need to understand how to run a business.

It's also true that those with a business background will in some ways have a leg up in this respect.

However, what I know to be the greater truth, is that it doesn't matter.

And that as you do the work of embracing Multiple Streams, you can release the perceived obstacle of 'not being a business person'.

Let me put it this way. How many people start new businesses every day, without a previous background as an entrepreneur? Thousands, right?

How many people go into something new without knowing anything about it? Tens of thousands.
The fact of the matter is many coaches drop out of the business of coaching because they lose sight of why they are doing it, not because they don't understand business.

Certainly some coaches drop because they just can't make it. And that's why you should read the chapter on Coaching Day Jobs closely.

But according to Dr. David Hawkins, author of "Power versus Force",

"One individual who lives and vibrates to the energy of optimism and a willingness to be nonjudgmental of others...will counterbalance the negativity of 90,000 individuals who calibrate at the lower weakening levels."

Now if that isn't a root underpinning of why coaches do what we do, I don't know what is.

Do whatever it is you have to stay connected to that.

In short, when it comes to coaches 'understanding how to run a business', I think the emphasis is being put on the wrong thing here.

Figure out what the deep, clean passion is behind your desire to earn a living as a coach. And connect steadfastly to that.

If you work hard and practice, you can learn, step by step, 'how to' run a business, as thousands of coaches and non-coaches do, each and every year.

It may take six months, and it may take years. In fact, it's safe to say that probably all of us will continue to learn how to run a business well, until the day we stop doing business.
But regardless of where you are in your learning, what I am here to tell you is that you can start now by learning 'on the job' by following the Multiple Streams approach.

The important thing is you CAN start earning income today.

Down the road, you get to decide if the small business life is for you.

For now, this is very important. Keep studying the biz of coaching.

And as much as you learn the business of coaching, stay as deeply plugged into the spirit of why you're in the coaching business.

Conversation Points

The eminent Richard Bolles, author of *"What Color is Your Parachute?"* has described Life Mission as, *"the place where your heart's deepest gladness and the world's greatest need intersect."*

Based on this, why do you coach? Why MUST you coach? (You can't help it? Why?) Use bullet points, stories, examples, sentences, or drawings. Keep a copy of these reasons in front of you as a touchstone.

Can you not coach? If you were not pursuing coaching as a calling, what would you do?

How can you continue to learn the business of coaching in a way that doesn't inhibit your passion for coaching itself? Who will you entrust your business education to? These can be coaches, organizations, books, or memberships.

The Money Game

The Money Game is a great way to bridge the gap between big picture mind set shifts and the day-to-day practicalities of building streams of income.

It's a tool that's been used successfully in every online business I've personally consulted with, large and small. In some of the largest companies, playing the 'Money Game' was a weekly discipline.

The thing is, it's such a simple game, it often comes across as mundane, and all sorts of people I share it with end up skipping it. They figure they 'get' it, and they don't need to 'do' it.
While you can 'get' the concept of the Money Game intellectually, there is something about going through the process of doing it that I'm inviting you to feel.

If you're open to it, you'll find your Money Games gives you benchmarks that serve as a lighthouse or North Star. You'll be able to keep steering in the right direction because of it.

So get out a pencil and a calculator, and as we go through it, play along. Later in the book you'll come back to the Money Game as your blueprint.

And as your plans and energy towards multiple streams ebb and flow as they naturally will, part of the beauty of the Money Game is that you'll be able to adjust, turn things up and turn things down. Just like the seasons come and go and it gets hotter or cooler over the course of the year.

Working and adapting your Money Game blueprint will keep you on course.
Ready?

Okay.

This involves some basic math. Really!

Get a copy of the Money Game Worksheet at
www.msoci.com/bulletins/moneygame.doc
(There is also a worksheet included at the end of this chapter)

First, fill in the blank with your name, so for example "Barb's Money Game" or "Bill's Money Game." Then fill in the date.

Next, for the purposes of this exercise, decide on a figure that we'll call your financial goals for the next 12 months. Fill that in.

Note, it doesn't matter if your goal is $100,000, $10,000, $10 million or $100 million, there's no right or wrong answer.

By the way, you can take some additional time later to refine this whole worksheet. I personally use an Excel spreadsheet which I really love working with, which you may like to try.

You'll be revisiting and refining the worksheet numerous times a year, and probably more like at least once a month if you are actively building your multiple streams. So don't worry about getting it 'precisely right.'

So you've filled in the number for your financial goals for the next 12 months, that's great.

Now sit back for a moment, and consider this number.

If we take the figure $120,000 as an example, thinking about building a coaching business to reach that number can be pretty daunting.

So instead what I'd like to do with you is highlight the fact that a multiple streams approach to achieving this goal is far easier to get your arms around.

The multiple streams approach captures a key secret that the most successful people know so well.

When you break down a single large financial goal into chunks, things instantly become more achievable and your chances of success are immediately much higher.

Consider this:

If 100 people pay $100 each month, that's $10,000 per month or $120,000 over the course of the year.

Pretty simple, right?

Now at this point as you've been reading along in the book, you may well be considering creating an information product as your first income stream. It's a great idea.

If that's the case you may be thinking, *"Hmm, 100 dollars per product, that's a little high priced for an e-Book, Andrea."*

Good, then this next sentence is for you.

If 100 people pay $39, that's $3900 per month or $46,800 over the course of the year.

$39 is a pretty reasonable and doable dollar figure for a well-positioned e-Book with a niche focus. I know most of us who've purchased things online would agree you see a wide range of prices for e-Books, starting from $9 for a tiny report, to $19, $27, $39, $49 and even $97 sometimes for e-Book type products.

So let's just say that $39 is not an unreasonable figure to work with.

And further to that, if you sell 100 copies of a $39 e-book each month, guess what? That grosses you almost 50,000 in one year from that one e-book.

If your one-year financial goal happens to be $150,000, then...you got it. You need to write three e-books at $39 apiece, and sell 100 copies each month in order to reach $150,000 for that year.

Not too bad.

Now all you have to do is write those e-Books right? No problem!

Okay, just to finish off with the rest of the Money Game, I know from experience working Money Games with one-on-one clients...

you probably have a very natural question at this point.

"Okay well yes, Andrea, I can see that $39 is a reasonable number, but the 100 people per month buying my e-book? That's a lot of people!"

To which of course, the answer is yes, you're right. If you're starting out it can seem like a lot of people.

So let's try one last statement in this sample Money Game we're playing.

Consider that:

If 50 (as compared with 100) people pay $39 per month, that's $1,950 each month or $23,400 over the course of the year.

NOTE: This is where the aspect of the money game comes in and powerfully shifts us into a bigger picture perspective.

You see, when forecasting the revenue for your coaching business using the multiple streams approach...you can use a slide rule for each of the pertinent numbers.

And for each of the numbers, you can experiment with putting the numbers you are most comfortable with.

So whether it's the number of people you project, anticipate or research tells you can scientifically expect to buy your product, OR

Whether it's the price tag that you would be comfortable pricing your material at,

You can shift those numbers up and down and until you end with a monthly gross revenue number as well as a yearly number that fits into the bigger picture of your yearly financial goals.

This may mean that you have 5 revenue streams, or 15. Or it could mean that you only have 3. Try it and see what you come up with, because the real magic of the Money Game is when you extrapolate it and personalize it.

Use the worksheets that follow this chapter to try it out for your unique set-up. By that I mean, the unique set of knowledge, experience and style in which you deliver your coaching message. Now, if we take the last statement...

If 50 people pay $39 each month, that equals $23,400 each year.

If you could write 6 e-books at that rate, and commit to getting the skills and knowledge you need to generate and convert enough traffic at your website in order to sell 50 e-books each month... voila. You have yourself $150,000 for that year.

Does this example help highlight how very doable that is?

It's about more than the mechanics of the math.

The Money Game and the Multiple Streams mindset is a way for you to reframe the way you look at earning coaching income. It's a way for you to be comfortable as you build the streams that work best for you in a way that fits your coaching business.

Are you more comfortable selling things at a lower price point perhaps? Hey that's just great. To increase your income, raise the number of people you reach with that price point.
Or maybe you feel you have a really powerful set of material and

you'd like to sell it for $100, $1000 or even $10,000 per piece. Great. Maybe you only need to sell 5 or 50 pieces to meet your goal.

Enjoy playing with the Money Game and the Multiple Streams formula.

Just remember that it is a formula, and that if you're wiling to re-frame your mind around this way of looking at things, it can make a coach's life a lot different on a day-to-day basis. That's you!

In fact, I'll go even further to say that as you start reframing your mind around this, you'll start realizing that multiple streams approach is the solution to one of the biggest myths I know of in the coaching indus-try, and that is that it's difficult to make a living as a coach.

UNTRUE.

Well, okay, let me take that back. It's true, if you think inside the box.

True if you're stubborn about coaching one-on-one being the only way you to make an impact and a living as a coach.

In that case, yes, for most people it's going to be hard to make a living as a coach if they're tied to that one-on-one way of doing business.

If you're willing to change your mind that you're going to think outside the box, and instead, study, integrate and embrace earning a living using a coaching approach, this all of a sudden becomes a completely different playing field for you.

Oh, one quick point of emphasis here:

An early version of the Money Game is *THE KEY TOOL* that I used on a weekly basis to build Thomas Leonard's different organizations into millions of dollars in less than 2 years.

It took me close to a year to realize its importance. You on the other hand, since you're reading about it here in this book...you don't need to waste any time. You can start using it right away.

Ready to extrapolate to your situation?

What are your financial targets and how can you break them down into do-able streams that together reach your yearly goal? Play around with the numbers and see what happens.

Up for it?

Good. As you open your revenue streams, you'll use the Money Game to keep you focused. You can create an Excel spreadsheet for it. You'll "work" the numbers. You'll delightedly watch the numbers get bigger.

Over time, this equals big money...which is just another way to say you're reaching a lot of clients. Bingo.

As you continue with the rest of the book or perhaps return to your work now, keep your eyes, ears and heart open.

See if you can "see" where opportunities for new revenue are showing up in your life right now. And start formulating where in *YOUR* Money Game they want to fit.

Make a note of it.

The Money Game Worksheet

Name:

Date:

My financial goals for the next 12 Months:

Statement One: If _____ people pay $_____ each month, that equals $_____ per month or $_____ per year.

Statement Two: If _____ people pay $_____ each month, that equals $_____ per month or $_____ per year, times _____ products equals $_____ per year.

Statement One: If _____ people pay $_____ each month, that equals $_____ per month or $_____ per year.

Statement Two: If _____ people pay $_____ each month, that equals $_____ per month or $_____ per year, times _____ products equals $_____ per year.

Statement One: If _____ people pay $_____ each month, that equals $_____ per month or $_____ per year.

Statement Two: If _____ people pay $_____ each month, that equals $_____ per month or $_____ per year, times _____ products equals $_____ per year.

Statement One: If _____ people pay $_____ each month, that equals $_____ per month or $_____ per year.

Statement Two: If _____ people pay $_____ each month, that equals $_____ per month or $_____ per year, times _____ products equals $_____ per year.

Statement One: If _____ people pay $_____ each month, that equals $_____ per month or $_____ per year.

Statement Two: If _____ people pay $_____ each month, that equals $_____ per month or $_____ per year, times _____ products equals $_____ per year.

Conversation Points

Chopping Wood, Carrying Water means practicing habits that help you carry out your bigger mission on a day-to-day basis. When the going gets hard for spiritual leaders, especially in the Zen tradition, they put a great deal of emphasis on going back to chopping wood and carrying water.

What everyday practical habits will help you make progress towards Multiple Streams of Coaching Income?

Using your results from the Money Game exercise, can you map out a general timeline for implementation of each of your streams?

What other ways can you gain clarity around making your money game a reality?

Apprenticing

Along the path from where you are now to millions in revenue, thousands in readers, tens of thousands of prospects, or hundreds of clients -- whatever criteria you use to define success for your coaching...there just is one key speed bump which is seldom talked about.

That is capacity.

This is especially true as your revenues grow up to six figures and you set your sights on building a seven-figure legacy business with a global impact.

How do you get your head around this problem? What secrets will ease your way through the growing pains?

In all the many thousands of hours of consulting, coaching and training I've done, there is only one key I've found to date that doesn't require significant cash investment. And that is the concept of apprentices.

The way I stumbled upon this was very personal. In 1993, my husband and I returned to Canada from Japan and decided to learn the craft of log home building.

We signed on with Pat Wolfe's Log Home Building School outside of Ottawa, Canada's National Capital.

Our agreement with him was this. For a not too small sum of several thousands of dollars, we would apprentice with him to build a real log home in 90 days.

In exchange he would show us the ropes, let us watch and shadow his technique; he would check our work, answer questions and generally guide us to completion in a way that would allow us to go to our own property and build our own home.

After we completed the learning, Pat turned around and sold the house to a waiting buyer for about 10% off the price of a house he built himself.

That was many years ago, but I remember clearly that there were multiple eager buyers for these student-built homes.

That's quite the business model isn't it?

It helps illustrate a great point. What you currently know - your knowledge and expertise, as well as what you are working on, would be a great education to many would-be entrepreneurs, coaches or other online hopefuls.

That's NOT 'only if you package it up' into a program or training module.

I mean 'just as you are, right now.'

In fact, I've toyed with the idea of having a training event in my home. I'd get up, stay in my pajamas and work on my streams of revenue. Perhaps open a new one. And all of you would shadow me.

It would be extremely expensive and only a few could come because my office isn't that big, but you'd learn a heck of a lot wouldn't you?

You'd probably have learned a lot following me around as I've completed this book.

The point is the same is true for you.

How you work, what you do, and why you do things the way you do, exactly as you do them right now, are valuable learning opportunities for your apprentices.
Several years ago I was one of those apprentices.

I'd been running my own recruitment business for some time, and had become disgruntled by putting great people into hierarchical organizations that stifled creativity and disregarded the whole person.

I decided to take a sabbatical and paid for supplies to begin volunteering with the Coaching Scoop's Real Interviews project for Steve Davis and Thomas Leonard of CoachVille.

Some might say I had found myself a real winner of an apprenticeship program.

I tell you this story for two reasons.

1. You may find yourself wishing for an apprenticeship for yourself, from time to time. It's a great way to move quickly into new areas by finding a mentor who will trade you a lifetime of wisdom for your legwork.

2. Regardless of where you think you 'are' in your work, you are ready for an apprentice. Because the benefits of an apprentice are in fact much greater to you than just the added pair of willing hands.

What you teach, you become.

And what you teach also becomes your legacy.

As you mentor your apprentices, there is a point at which they become your protégés.

This is a tipping point that occurs when the apprentice graduates from learning to creating.

At first, a gosling follows its mother to learn what to do when winter comes. It stays close, it imitates, it mimics. It never strays too far.

Once that young goose has served its apprenticeship, it graduates to flying on its own. It now creates a life of its own, informed by what it has learned from its mother.

In the business setting, powerful lessons can be learned by applying what works in nature. When you surround yourself with apprentices, it becomes very likely that you will discover some protégés. Apprentices will increase your capacity for work, but protégés will condition your heart to the bigger job of leaving your legacy, which we talk about in the next chapter.

A few things to bear in mind as you prepare for apprentices:

1. Don't change what you do.

Design the apprentice relationships so that it doesn't disrupt your productivity. Allow your apprentice to come into your existing set up. The key at the beginning is to increase your capacity, not add capacity.

Your apprentice is someone you invite to your house without cleaning up first. Soon enough, they'll be helping you tidy things.

2. Pick certain people for your apprentices. There are two main criteria.

You must like and respect them.

They should be entrepreneurially minded, meaning either they have run a business of their own OR they were brought up by family who did.

The latter covers just about every other characteristic you could want: loyalty, hard work, a sense of urgency, and a problem solving orientation.

3. Use technology and systems to support the addition of new people to your business.

The most basic and essential way to induct an apprentice is to set up a system of shadowing. The simplest way is to set up your email so that a copy gets sent to your apprentice.

Or, if you have some mail you wish not to share yet, make it a discipline to blind carbon copy every email you wish them to see. As you reply, manage and complete tasks, your apprentice will model you, and task by task, take over for you.

The shadowing technique allows them to learn your voice, timing and judgment calls in a very efficient way.

Once you feel they can give it a try, flip the switch and have the apprentice blind carbon copy you so you can check their work for a period of time before they go solo.

One word of caution: As you try training some apprentices for the first time, you will experience some churn. It may take several tries before you find someone who will stick with you.

That's a natural part of the selection process because the apprentice – mentor relationship can rely quite a bit on personal chemistry and whether or not the visions align.

By using technology well, adding a great apprentice or two can feel a lot like adding massive horsepower to what used to run like a motorized scooter.

In doing so, you add a structure to your business that will pull you forward to the next level of play, both in terms of the volume of work you can complete, and in the emotional commitment to greatness that happens when other people start watching you and learning from you.

Along your path to multiple streams of all the revenue you want, I wish you a smooth drive with speed bumps you are prepared for!

Conversation Points

In my opinion, every fully functioning coach has someone behind them that they are 'bringing along.' An apprentice or protégé. In addition, they have someone ahead of them that they are following. This is their mentor.

And lastly, they have someone beside them, who is their coach.

Who are the people in your life right now who are serving these functions? These people are your success environment. If you don't have a protégé, mentor or coach, what will you do now to commit to getting one?

If you do have one, how are the relationships going? Can you acknowledge, give thanks to or expand the relationship somehow?

What do you know right now, that would be valuable for some-one else to learn? Not learn from a book perspective, but from a hands-on perspective?

If I had one or more apprentices working with me 10 hours a week, what would I ask them to do?

What are three reasons I may be holding back from finding an apprentice, and why?

As I create a plan for Multiple Streams of Coaching Income, how can I design an offering that adds apprentices to my business AND brings in revenue?

Come As You Are

Don't Change a Thing.

As I've worked with the Charter Members of Multiple Streams of Coaching Income, here's another issue that has come up quite a bit.

"But Andrea, I don't have anything to offer in an information product."

Pfffft.

Here's the thing. Have you ever read something that you've read a dozen times in other places, but this one time you read it, it hits you on the head like a sack of apples?

What is it about that one time?

Why did it hit you, when the other times the same information was presented, it didn't?

It's this little thing that goes like this:

Some things, some people can only hear from you.

Why do you think the Bible was written from four different perspectives by people who witnessed the same events: Matthew, Mark, Luke and John?

Or that some people resonated with the story of King Arthur only when it was told from the women's point of view in Marion Zimmer Bradley's *"Mists of Avalon"*?

It's all perspective.

By coming as you are, and writing your e-books, producing your workshops, and recording your audios, from exactly where you are, you are handing people the most valuable gift you can give someone. Because somewhere out there, people are waiting for you to present your material in a way that makes sense to them.

I used to get confused when I saw that two competing services both got rave reviews. How to choose between them? Until I realized that, of course, different people will be attracted to different methods of delivery and style.

I used to get paralyzed by information overload...there are so many products out there, how could it possibly be beneficial for me to add to the heap?

When creating your offerings, take a moment to get clear about your value, and what you have to offer. And do what it takes for you to come as you are.

No need to study up and 'get smart' first, before you create something. Re-read the chapter in the marketing section entitled 'Human Googles' and remember that people are not looking for more information, they're looking for the precise information they need at that given moment.

All you need to do is filter it and add value to that information based on your life experience. Share your story, your successes and your challenges. Make your unique connections.

A good way to practice showcasing the value of exactly where you are is blogging or journaling. Although a blog needs to have a strong business tie-in to produce profits for you, it is a fantastic personal development tool for coaches who want to learn how to create products quickly.

Each blog post should be personal, but tie back to the business value of the story. By all means share the fact that someone asked you to take a photo of them today with a cell phone camera, but tie it back to the fact that this is viral marketing at its best.

There are examples of 'coming as you are' all around us if you care to notice.

One of my favorites is the story of Destiny's Child, the music group led by Beyonce Knowles. When trouble kept on dogging her, she came out with the single *"I'm a Survivor!"* which went to and stayed right at the top of the charts.

Beyonce had the guts to come just as she was, and the emotional truth of that resonated and ricocheted into millions of sales.

As one of my mentors says, *"Your mess is your message."*

Use your journal or blog to practice drawing out the message in your life, whether it's messy or not, and you'll find the creative process a much more freeing experience.

Conversation Points

What three challenging events in your history – and your triumphs - could you share with others to good effect?

If you think you've considered this before, try again, dig deeper. You have more to offer and more streams of income in you waiting to be tapped than you might think.

What stuck places are you in right now that you could document and describe in the form of a coaching product? Are you trying to lose weight? Breaking off a relationship? Raising a daughter?

In what ways might you be pretending to be someone you are not, in your work and relationships? How can you release those masks and move towards more brutal honesty and integrity in your life?

If You're A Student of Music, You Must Listen To Music

Before continuing, A <u>Must</u> For new and veteran coaches:

If you're brand new as a coach, you're lucky. Don't think of yourself as 'behind' or 'needing to catch up.'

In some key ways, you are actually 'ahead.'

You don't have a ton of baggage to drop before you embrace the principles in this book. Go for it and don't let anyone hold you back.

Regardless of where you are at, what I want to emphasize to you is the one thing I hope you get out of this book if you get nothing else.

Just because this book is all about how to earn money as a coach, doesn't mean you can afford to ignore this.

Because that would be like an athlete trying to get into the Olympics without drinking 8 glasses of water each day.

Or like a virtuoso violin player who never listened to music.

Coaches, take your own medicine -- get a coach.

Work on who you are, the leadership role you want to play in your life, for your family, for your community, for yourself.

Then tell the world about it and go about the business of building multiple streams of income so you can proudly call yourself a financially successful coach.
Otherwise, my dear coaching friend, I would hazard to say that coaching will remain just a hobby to you.

Remember hobbies are things you spend money *on*. Businesses and careers are things you earn money *from*.

By having a coach yourself, you are practicing one of the very most neglected, and the very most important criteria for being a coach.

I haven't done a poll on this, but I think I'd be frightened to know the real truth. The majority of coaches do not have a coach themselves.

Be different.

Practice being an awesome coaching client.

The added dimension to this is that it serves very well as market research. Try on several coaches for pay, or buddy coaches for free, group coaching opportunities, email coaching at discussion lists, etc.

Finances are a poor reason for not having a coach. Just go get one who will help you get your finances in order so you can afford their help.

Practice being a very motivated coaching customer, work on your wants and needs and desires for your own ideal life.

In doing so, you'll be in integrity in a way that's critical to becoming financially successful yourself.

Until you get coached, you'll never be a top-drawer coach.

Put this book down, and take three steps now towards getting a coach for yourself.

Already got one? Good.

Go find another one for another aspect of your life, whether that is finances, writing, family, a hobby, anything. Try another style or mode of coaching, in groups, a gym or something else. Your 'first' coach won't mind.

In fact, if they are a great coach, they're doing the same thing, learning and accelerating their greatness by surrounding themselves with many people who are positively impacting their lives.

Practice being a fantastic coaching client.

Conversation Points

What constitutes a terrific coaching client, in your opinion? Are you a great coaching client?

Take some time each week between sessions with your coach to listen to music that inspires and energizes you. Music unlocks energy. And there is plenty of music that coaches, if you'd like to call it that, starting with this list.

What songs can you add to the list?

(Thank you to Coach Reslie Costabell of Costabell.com for compiling this list at the Euro-Coach Forum.)

- *True Colours*, Cyndi Lauper
- *Could You be Loved*, Bob Marley
- *Miracle of Love*, Eurythmics
- *Money Can't Buy It*, Annie Lennox
- *Born to be Wild*, Steppenwolf
- *Climb Every Mountain*, The Sound of Music
- *Up*, Shania Twain
- *Moving on Up*, M People
- *Who Wants To Live Forever?* Queen
- *We are the Champions* - Queen
- *What the World Needs Now is Love*, Jackie DeShannon
- *The Circle of Life*, Elton John
- *My Way*, Frank Sinatra
- *I Can See Clearly Now*, Johnny Nash
- *Ain't got no -- I got Life*, Nina Simone
- *You Can't Always Get What You Want*, Rolling Stones
- *If I Were a Rich Man*, Topol
- *Raise a Little Hell* – Trooper

Conclusion

Are You Ready To Be a Leader NOW?

My favorite quote about leadership is this:

"It often happens that I wake up at night and begin to think about a serious problem and decide...'I must tell the Pope about it.' Then I wake up completely and remember that I am the Pope."

–Pope John XXIII

Another less known quote on personal leadership is one I share from an instant message conversation in the summer of 2002, before the CoachVille Corporate Coaching Conference held in Toronto in September...

"I think I might be ready to be a leader now..."

–Thomas J. Leonard

There has been just so much written on the topic of leadership. I presume in this brief conclusion to say nothing more than a few words which I hope will cause you to recognize the leader that you are.

Both quotes above indicate something in their own way. There is a leader inside each of us, not waiting to come out so much, as patiently waiting to be acknowledged.

Coaches, at heart, are leaders. And leaders, in fact, good ones...are coaches.

There is a Coaching Solution for Every Problem and it's up to you now to make those solutions happen.

That's your mission if you choose to accept it.

The Multiple Streams approach to earning a living is working for thousands right now. The tools and techniques of internet and direct marketing give you the means to reach the world.

You can start by joining other Multiple Streams coaches who are already proving this first hand.

You can continue by having deeper conversations about this whole idea with as many others as you can.

Whether they are mentors, protégés, fellow coaches, your coach, your family or friends. What I hope you'll do with the ideas in this book is expand them. Adapt them. Critique them. Make them work. Evolve them.

Because as you and the tens of thousands of other coaches do that, we'll hit the tipping point in no time.

Welcome to the new game of coaching. This is the Multiple Streams Game where the possibilities for wealth and legacy are huge.

Are you ready to take the lead?

I'm sure those of you who knew Thomas Leonard's work can feel the humor and pathos in what he said about leadership.

When I read his words, I had myself a 'moment' and said a prayer of thanks.

It was a breakthrough for him.

I was so glad he stepped into the shoes he didn't know he'd already been walking in. Even for just a year, he consciously lived life as the leader he was.

It's my opinion that one of the most profound pieces of writing he created was the 15 Proficiencies of Modern Leadership which remain housed in the Graduate School of Coaching.

These 15 Proficiencies are my yardstick for my work. Have a look at them on page 9 at this attributed link:
http://www.andreajlee.com/thomas.html

> *"You wander from room to room*
> *Hunting for the diamond necklace*
> *That is already around your neck!"*
>
> – Jalal-Uddin Rumi

Are you ready to acknowledge the diamond necklace around your neck?

Are you, like the beloved John XXIII, ready with wry humor to look to yourself instead of others, for leadership?

Are you ready to coach and be the leader that you are, now?

Say yes, because it's time. Time for coaches to take the mantle of leadership.

Get started by taking care of your business by working on your streams of income. And onward from there.

Conversation Points

What will it take for you to step out into your leadership now, this minute, in the big and little things that you do?

How will you continue to nurture your study of leadership, what it means to you, how it manifests in your life every day?

What commitment will you make to facing self-doubt with courage, and recognize that someone in the world is waiting for your gifts?

How long will you keep them waiting?

Epilogue

Thank you for reading this book.

In it, I hope you've caught a sense of the bigger game in store for coaches.

As mentioned in the beginning of the book, with the thoughts contained in these pages I'm sure we can lovingly repot our concept of Coaching in a way that it flourishes.

I hope you embrace the invitation to become a coach who thinks in Multiple Streams.

If you'd like to continue the conversation in a supportive environment where I share thoughts and ideas on how to make money and meaning as a coach and business owner, I encourage you to visit my blog at **www.MoneyandMeaningBlog.com**

I'll be sharing the latest news and information with all the coaches there, and actively looking forward to your contributions.

Next Steps: How Can I Build my Multiple Streams Business?

If the idea of building a Multiple Streams Business appeals to you, here are a couple of options to consider as next steps:

Since 2003, this little 'paperback-book-that-could' you are holding in your hands has been sold in the thousands around the world, and we're pleased now to offer the Multiple Streams Implementation Workbook as a companion guide. This is a streamlined step-by-step program emphasizing how to implement the Multiple Streams Product Funnel, simply, easily and sustainably.

You can begin by creating your first 'Pink Spoon' or use the same process to develop your signature 'big ticket product.' You'll find coaching questions on almost every page and space for your work. Note: This is a workbook to engage with up close, not just read.

You can find the Multiple Streams Implementation Workbook along with other products to grow your coaching business at: **www.MSOCI.com/Store**

Or, if you would like 'hands on' support to help you build your business you may want to consider hiring a Multiple Streams Coach.

The Multiple Streams Coaching Team is the ONLY coaching team in existence dedicated to building businesses based on the Multiple Streams of Coaching Income model, as brought to life in this book. Each member of the Multiple Streams Coaching Team has hands-on experience building businesses using the product funnel and 8 step process of the Multiple Streams model.

To get started with a Multiple Streams Coach go to: **www.MultipleStreamsCoaching.com**

And last but not least, be sure to get your copy of the FREE Award Winning Ecourse 'The Five Keys To Putting Money in Coaches' Pockets' at **www.MoneyForCoaches.com**, along with our regular publication 'Creating What Matters' for Business Owners who make a difference for a living, published twice a month.

You can also view—and register for—coaching and entrepreneur-ial-related classes and resources at **www.AndreaJLee.com**

Appendices

APPENDIX ONE:

The 8 Key Steps to Creating a Multiple Streams Product Funnel of Your Very Own

1. **Discover Your Niche Market,** also known as a group of people with common issues or concerns, that 'hang out' together. Your niche market enables you to access 'invisible' pockets of clients using the Funnel model...

2. **Elicit the Problems** being experienced most vividly by this group of people..."What's keeping them awake at night?" Use your innate abilities as a coach to ask and listen CLOSELY to what the market is saying.

3. **Find the Solutions** to the problems being expressed. This will be through a combination of your own knowledge and judicious research and surveying.

4. **Choose Your Packaging,** according to your personal strengths and preferences. Are you a verbal person? Do you like to write? We'll show you how to repackage and repurpose so you get multiple products from one set of content...

5. **Generate Traffic with integrity,** using proven low-tech, low-budget methods the internet marketers teach for thousands of dollars!

6. **Continue to Convert Traffic into Prospects,** at increasingly high percentages, using intimacy, mystery, sensuality and your growing gift for deepening and strengthening relationships.

7. **Feed Your Reservoir assertively and diligently.** The more you attract individuals to the top (or widest) part of the Product Funnel, the more accelerated your success will be in the other layers.

8. **Pursue a Bold, Outrageous, Provocative Position in your Niche Market.** Figure out what you believe in, and take a stand, working at all times on your authenticity and integrity. Your business success IS a reflection of your personal mastery. Important!

By putting into play EACH of these critical elements for your coaching business, you'll find the Multiple Streams Product Funnel a useful, doable and enjoyable new way of playing BIG(GER) as a coach.

Appendix Two:

So How Long Will This Take Me To Build? The Multiple Streams Timeline

What is the realistic expectation for starting an online Multiple Streams business from scratch, to getting cash flow from online products? 3 months? 6 months? A year? What are the steps at each stage? And how much money could we realistically expect to make at each stage?

It is important for Multiple Streams Coaches to be prepared for the time it actually takes to build their business, and set reasonable goals and expectations when it come to generating revenue from online products.

And so we created the 'Timeline to Cashflow Online'...

This is a step by step outline of how to start a Multiple Streams business from scratch - the steps to setting up a pink spoon page, working through the funnel, what kind of investment to make along the way and what kind of return can be expected.

First, note that of course, this is just a template. There is always room to go faster or slower through the timeline, or to mix things up a bit. Some hop to Phase 3 in a month, others may take up to a year to really get going. You can go at your own pace - that's the beauty of the Product Funnel model.

So let's take a look at the three phases of the timeline - for simplicity sake, I've indicated a month by month timeline, as if you were to start January 1st.

Phase 1: Problem/Solution
0 - 3 months (Jan - Mar)
Revenue: 0

This is the stage where you define who your market is. Who do you want to help? What are their biggest problems? Do the research and get in touch the biggest issues your market is facing. One of the best ways to do this is to simply ask them - do an online survey with the question 'What is your biggest challenge?'

From this information you can build your first 'one-banana' website, offering a free gift (pink spoon) in exchange for their email address.

Phase 2: Driving Traffic (Honk Honk!)
4 - 6 months (Apr - June)
Revenue: 0
List: 500 - 1000 people

You have a website, you have a free gift. Now you need to start driving traffic to your site so you can build your list of names/email addresses.

It is important to build your relationship as you build your list. Keep in regular touch with people through a newsletter or series of autoresponders. Be engaging and helpful, and keep asking questions. Provide them value while also providing them an opportunity to get to know you. People buy from people that they know, like and trust.

Phase 3: Show me the Money
7 - 12 months (July - Dec)
Revenue: $500 - $1500+/month
List: 1000 - 2000+ people

Once you have gotten to know your market, identified their problems, built trust, etc, it is time to start selling them products that will help solve their problems. E-books and/or TeleSeminars are a great place to start.

After 6 months of research, driving traffic and building a relationship with your list, it would not be unreasonable to start making $500 - $1000/month. For example, if you sell a TeleSeminar at $97 with 20 spots you've made $2000 right there (and more for selling the audio later). Or if you offer an e-book for $27 and you sell 50 copies, that's another $1350.

Phase 3 doesn't have an end date, unless you pull the plug. Continue to talk to the people on your list, keep in touch with what they want and create products that they want to buy as you move through the Funnel.

APPENDIX THREE:

The Most Common Problems Humans Experience

Stuck in a Rut
Not Enough Time
Not Enough Money
Lack of Confidence
Fear of Unknown
Not knowing what they want
Not understanding
Miscommunicating
Fear of Conflict
Inability to say no
Relationships that sap
Too much money
Lack of Organization
Boredom
Unclear goals
Unsupporting Family
A Job they hate
Scattered focus
Superiority Complex
Lack of courage
Running on Adrenaline
Workaholism
Weak Boundaries
Lack of Vision
Negativity
Overweight
Fear of Success
Poor people management skills

Poor money management skills
Poor communication skills
Pressure from Work
Not self aware
No definition of personal success
Unhappy relationship
Lack of Relationship
Lack of love
Low self-awareness
Overreactions
Lack of Energy
Lack of Technical Know How
Detached from Community

APPENDIX FOUR:

The Many Different Coaching Formats

E-books

Mini-E-books

Ecourses or Course by Email

Web-based training

Print books

TeleSeminars, Single

TeleSeminars, Program based

Licenses for your programs or other content

Live Workshops and Seminars

Live Conferences

Live Conference Coaching

Keynote and Speaking Engagements

Sell or Resell Technology

Sell or Resell Systems and Tools

Create Software

Group Coaching, via Phone

Group Coaching, via Discussion Board

Group Coaching, via Discussion List

Web-based Audio Recordings

CDs/Audio Tapes

Web-based Video Recordings

Videos/DVDs

Multimedia Training

Membership Websites and portals

Web-based training

Feeder Coaching Programs for Books

Feeder Coaching Programs for Conferences

Feeder Coaching Programs for Schools

Businesses in a Box
Coaching and non-coaching "Day Jobs"
Coaching Programs for Corporate Employers
Group Coaching by Webinar
Coaching Gyms
Consulting Services
Vendor Services for Coaching Industry
Gifts and Hard Goods for Coaching Industry
Motivational Gifts and Hard Goods
Website Advertising
EBay Products and Services
Joint venture partnerships
Affiliate Program Promotions
Affiliate Program Offerings
Coaching Radio Show
Coaching Television Show
Coaching Magazine
Coaching Newspaper
Writing assignments across all media

Coach the Coach programs for Niche Markets

Some of the above are better suited than others to the coaching skill set and mindset, as well as to where you are in your development as a businessperson.

Appendix Five:

A Working List of Niche Markets

Niche markets are everywhere, and there is both art and science to determining the best ones.

Remember that if you see a product selling itself as the magic bullet to choosing a niche market, you'll want to check when it was created.

Niche markets, like the news on TV, change rapidly, and you're better off investing your money elsewhere.

Here is a working list of evergreen Niche markets that you can use as a jumping off point. Always do up-to-date research to make sure of you don't invest time and energy into a too-competitive niche, or one that won't sustain you.

Plumbers
Acupuncturists
Authors
Daycare Centers
Tree house lovers
Teachers
Social Workers
Restaurant owners
Fitness Centers
Single Mothers
Personal Trainers
Talent Agents
Beauty Pageant Hopefuls

Accountants

Lawyers

Insurance Companies

Breast-feeding Mothers

Photographers

Organic Food Eaters

Newbie to Technology

Chefs

Manufacturers

Guinea Pig Owners

Mortgage Brokers

Veterinarians

Human Resource Professionals

Magicians

Disc Jockeys

Comedians

Financial Planners

Harmonica Players

Virtual Assistants

Parents of Twins

English as a Second language speakers

Physicians

Surgeons

Hairdressers

Chiropractors

MAC users

Interior Designers

Web designers

Dentists

Teenaged Boys

Police

New York City Firefighters

Emergency Workers

Programmers
Athletes in various sports
Actors
Motivational Speakers
Realtors
Chowhounds
Electric Guitar Players
Day Spa Owners
Pastors
Administrative Assistants
Women CEOs
Military Fathers
Silver Spoon Collectors
Fly fishermen
Florists
Soccer enthusiasts
Divorced fathers
War Veterans
Vegetarians
Women over 6 ft.

To identify additional niche markets, write down descriptors of you, your friends and family. What niches do you belong to that may be worth researching for your business?

APPENDIX SIX:

Sample Ecourse Issue

'The Five Keys to Putting Money in Coaches' Pockets' brought to you by Multiple Streams of Coaching Income Author Andrea J. Lee.

Issue One of Five

Dear Coach,

Welcome to this ecourse that's been written to shift your mindset.

Some concepts may be new to you, some may not. I invite you to play the process and read through either way, with the intent that you finish the ecourse in five days with a different way of looking at money for you, a coach. None of the emails is overly long, so give yourself the gift of focus and set aside five minutes to read each one.

You've gone so far as to sign up for the mini-course, now I invite you to reap the full benefit of it. The exercises at the end of each email are interactive; you are invited to participate by sending your answers by hitting reply.

Although we may not answer every email, each one is read and filed confidentially so you can use this course as an environment that pulls you forward, should you wish.

Enjoy.

Key #1: Understand FULLY that you can't give away what you don't have.

If you want to be generous, you must be wealthy. If you want to be attractive, you must have plenty. If you want to change lives, you must have reserve.

If you want to be a coach, you must be coachable.

In other words, stop being wishy-washy about money. Make sure you are sure, in no uncertain terms, that you want to be a financially well-off, actively practicing coach.

There is no shame in this. You are a model for others. Model prosperity on all levels, and don't fatally short-change yourself or your clients by being 'ho-hum' about money.

This includes, *"I'm not doing this for the money."*
"I want to earn money but more important is that I am changing lives and enjoying what I do."

And all other variations. You know the kind!

This is the art of holding seemingly conflicting intentions. Helping others and being financially wealthy are simply not mutually exclusive. It can be done. What you do, by embracing this key shift, is recognize that a continuous struggle with money is just an unhealthy as an obsession with becoming rich.

The first key to putting money in your pocket occurs when you become willing to say, "I want to be a financially wealthy coach."

Exercise: 99% of humans, coaches included, have angst over money

Earning it, spending it, and accumulating wealth. Research shows that until and unless money becomes a non-issue...ie. no longer a struggle...human beings never move beyond struggle... to do what could be done.

What are your money issues and what will you commit to, to address and evolve beyond them?

Ask, "What could I do in my life, if money was absolutely no longer an issue?"

Now, make a plan to pursue this possibility. Hit reply to share and diarize your thoughts if you wish. To get a copy of your own reflections, just add your email address as well, and you'll have your own record for future reference.

Now just hang on until tomorrow and I'll ask you to address a truly fundamental piece of the puzzle when it comes to money and coaches...

With love and respect,

Andrea Lee, Author | Multiple Streams of Coaching Income
andrea@andreajlee.com | **www.andreajlee.com**

P.S. To Get a Copy of the Book and become one of a growing number of Multiple Streams Coaches, visit:
www.MultipleStreamsofCoachingIncome.com

----

end issue one, sign up for the remaining issues at **www.msoci.com**

About the Author

ANDREA J. LEE is an award-winning author, entrepreneur, mentor, coach and consultant to business owners on five continents.

A thought-leader in the field of personal and business coaching, she built and managed the largest coach training company and network in the world.

Now the CEO of the Andrea J. Lee Group of Companies, she writes, speaks and develops advanced marketing, internet and business systems for coaches.

Her mission?

To put money in the pockets of 10,000 coaches by 2008.

Recognized for her leadership by McGill University's Scarlet Key Society, her company was named by Seth Godin and Fast Company Magazine as one of the extraordinary 'Bull Market' companies helping their clients stand out and prosper.

Andrea currently lives in Calgary, Alberta, Canada with her husband of nine years, Michael James Flannery and their two Vizslas named Chili and Eureka.

Getting in Touch/Getting More Involved

You are wholeheartedly welcome to get in touch with Andrea and the Multiple Streams of Coaching Income team.

This could be for any of the following reasons:

- To ask any question.
- To provide feedback.
- To join in to help evolve the coaching profession.
- To volunteer for a multiple streams project, training or other endeavor.
- To find out where Andrea will be speaking next.
- To receive updates about multiple streams, including new book titles planned for next year.
- To inquire about joint ventures or joining the coaching team.
- Something else entirely.

By email: **support@andreajlee.com**

By website: **www.MultipleStreamsofCoachingIncome.com**
Or **www.AndreaJLee.com/blog**

By mail: Suite 152, 1919B - 4 Street SW | Calgary, AB T2S 1W4 Canada

By phone: 1 (403) 615-1237 mountain standard time

By message in a bottle: Throw hard and set a great big intention!

Additional Website References from within the pages of the Book

To spread the word about the book via email, visit:
www.MSOCI.com/tellafriend.html

To get recommendations for systems, tools and resources that will help you build your own Multiple Streams, visit:
www.AndreaRecommends.com

For more info about Coaching Programs in a Box, visit:
www.MSOCI.com/cpib

For more info about the trial membership available to book readers only, visit: **www.MSOCI.com/bookreadersonly**

Acknowledgments

- All the very special early adopting Multiple Streams Members, Internet Biz Whizzers, and readers of the blog.
- All the one-on-one coaching clients I've been privileged to serve and learn from.
- All the dear early members of CoachVille and the Schools of Coaching
- My many mentors and coaches.

These people in particular, in their own various ways, have helped supported the creation, built the buzz and exemplified the values in this book:

Curious who they are? Here you go:

Mike Flannery, Jan MacGregor, Tina Forsyth, Kerri Martin, Lable Braun, Susan Austin, Valerie Green, Anna Dargitz, Kelli McCauley, Richard Reardon, Nina East, Irwin Lee, Edward Lee, H. George and Julie Lee, Jillian Middleton, Rose Hill, Mitch Axelrod, Thomas Leonard, Ericka Loften, Lena West, Sandy Vilas, David Goldsmith, Shirley Anderson, Bryan Yambao, Kim Black, Brian Platz, Tom Heck, Joel and N'Omi Orr, Seth Godin, Ken McArthur, Ken McCarthy, Perry Marshall, Roger Montgomery, Chris Barrow, Bob Silber, Willie Crawford, Esther Beris, David Flack, Marie Kane, Alicia Smith, Lynne and Larry Klippel, Sue Thomson, David Stowell, Dan Morris, Dan Roberge, Candye Hinton, Jack Brown, Peggy Champlin, Steve Stockton, Dave Wood, Milana Leshinsky, Sylva Leduc, Stacy Morales, Marion Franklin, Bernadette Morando, Sharilyn Horne, Ken Winston Caine, Ben Graham, Jim Vuocolo, Katie Darden, Nicola Cairncross, Guy Levine, Dave Buck, Lee

Weinstein, Steve Davis, Mary Lewis, Dan Janal, Susan Harrow, John Satta, Maria Andreu, Gail Stone, Leslie Nielsen, Anne Ryan, Anne Tyrie, Anne Wondra, Bob Cobb, Barry Zweibel, BS Chew, Coop Cooper, Susan Chapman, Donna Karlin, Deborah Brown, Jules Charest, James 'Milo' Milojkovic, Jimm Hughey, Judy Irving, Ken Zaretsky, Kerry and Kristelle Sim, Maralyn Cale, Susie Leonard, Judy Feld, Marki Talley, Marijo Hayes, Cheryl Miller, Natalie Miller, Noel Evans, Rey Carr, Ruth Ledesma, Steve Latham, Sunny Hills from Maui, Vicky White, Vikki Brock, Jeff Wasserman, Barry Silverman, Michael Port, Hal Macomber, Dovid Grossman, Sid Smith, Jennifer Corbin, Elsom Elridge, Judy Murdoch, Laurie and Jon Weiss, Merlyn Sanchez, Douglas Emerson, Colleen Larson, Noranne Dickin, Judith Buddle, Laura Hendershot, Dan Forsyth, Leslie Male, Sherri Olsen, Ray Lamb, Barbara Calkins, Ernest Oriente, Rhonda Rogers, PeeWee the Clown, Chris Hutchison, Liz Westbury, Jim Pender, Robert Alderman, Linda Oprica, Ashish Pawaskar, Jan Solomita, Sali Taylor, Kerul Kassel, Scott Stratten, Wayne Jones, Roger Son of Wilma DeWitt, Naomi Tickle, Peter Schneider, Jennifer Haver, Maria Marsala, Lotta Alsen, Maryam Webster, Catherine Lee, Sheila Martin, Ramon Williamson, Jennifer Haver, Obejoyful Lynd, Nitu Gandhi, Lewis Downey, Cindy Greenway, Tonya Signa, Robet Alderman, Blair Hornbuckle, Pamela Richarde, Michael Green, Wayne Jones, Christopher Knight, Coen de Groot, Lisa Micklin, Sunny Hills, CJ Hayden, Dan Poynter, Des Walsh, Marcia Bench, Patsi Krakoff, Laurie and Jon Weiss, Pam Love, Nancy Boyd, Sharon Hooper, Leslie Cardinal, Linda Dessau, James Flaherty, Phil Humbert, Andy Wibbels, Julia Stewart, Patricia Soldati, Bob Trainor, Suzan Fiskin, Ann Griffiths, Rob Huston, Teresia LaRocque, Sue Bond, Stephen Fairley, Sylvia Warren, Manfred Laube, Donna Rougeau, Paul Low, Jean-Pierre LeBlanc, Karen Mulligan, Don McAvinchey, Jayne Harper, Annie Kaszina, Gary Vurnum, Sarah Newton, Marty Crouch, Vickie Lewis, Judy Mason, Molly Luffy, Lisa McElmurry, Ivan Dietschener, Bob Silber, Sharilyn Horne, Alex Mandossian, Mike Jay, Laura and Simon Reilly, Gavin Allison, Leslie Geibhart, Andii Lindsay, Kay Malone, Susan Fuller, Karla Guleserian, Nick Crane, Diane Krause, Kimberly Sobie, Heather Waring, Jennifer Koretsky, Pat Snow, Debbie Roening, Alison Zecha, Val Williams, Donna Lendzyk, Barbara Lemaire, Barbra Sundquist, Daina Puodzuinas, Emily Bouchard, Vicky White, Larry Face, Ebbie Willis, Jayne Sorrels, Trudy Arthurs, Lora Adrianse, Fabienne Frederickson, Liberty Craig, Martin Hogg, David Stocum, Don Morris, Lori Richardson, Helen McClagish, Kim Nishida, Lorraine Powell, Michelle Huse, Ruth Ann Harnisch, Shantel McBride, Soni Pitts, Carol Gerrish, Lisa Kirshner, Lisa Hardin, Mr. & Ms. Kerry Sim, Barbara Calkins, Aeriol Nicols, Mary Anderson, Greg and Tracey Fieber, Viveca Monehan, Barry Zweibel, Phyllis Reid-Moore, Kim Lapp, Peter Schneider, Peter Cook, Bill Astalnok, Lorna Minewiser, Barry Wilverman, Jan Marie Dore, Lynne Colwell, Len Kaplan, Jessie Hipolit, Katherine Gotshall English, Matt Perelstein, Julie Inman, Shari Carr, Cheryl Simpson, Kurt Vander Weg, Stasia Carr, Janet Earls, Rosemary Hauschild, Iris Marchaj, Stephanie Dalfonzo, Al Cannistraro, Judy Sabah, Ernie Moore

And of course:

Lynne and Larry Klippel, the intrepid Book Shepherding team at FemmeOsagePublishing.com, my eternal gratitude.

Tina Forsyth for her steadfast, unabashed and early support and encouragement; and Kerri Martin, for her willingness and dedication through thick and thin.